"I Never Did Learn to Dance"

(Confessions of an Interloper)

T. ARNOLD SPEARS

Copyright © 2013 by T. Arnold Spears
First Edition – October 2013

ISBN
978-1-4602-2362-8 (Paperback)
978-1-4602-2363-5 (eBook)

All rights reserved.

No part of this publication may be reproduced in any form, or by any means, electronic or mechanical, including photocopying, recording, or any information browsing, storage, or retrieval system, without permission in writing from the publisher.

Cover art by Elsa Spears at age five. Used by permission.

Produced by:

FriesenPress
Suite 300 – 852 Fort Street
Victoria, BC, Canada V8W 1H8

www.friesenpress.com

Distributed to the trade by The Ingram Book Company

Acknowledgements:

To Nancy Foreman and Colin Anderson for patiently proofreading sections of the draft material and making many helpful suggestions; to André Bujold for kindly piloting the project through the intricacies of preparation for publication; to the staff at FriesenPress for their patient assistance and practical suggestions; and especially to my wife Joan for patiently sitting alone while I absented myself at the computer: to all of these my sincere gratitude! The warts and wrinkles that remain are my responsibility entirely.

Cover Art:
by Elsa Spears, at age five

Please note:
Unless otherwise indicated, Scripture references are taken from the HOLY BIBLE, NEW INTERNATIONAL VERSION© 1073, 1078, 1984 by International Bible Society. Used by permission of Zondervan Publishing House. All rights reserved.

Dedication:

To Elsa,
Who since her arrival on this scene some years ago
has been not only a joyous challenge to her mom and dad
but also a sheer delight to her doting Granny and Mumpa 'the Vet'
providing a brilliant sparkle to the snows of our winter!

"*The LORD bless you and keep you;*
The LORD make His face shine upon you
And be gracious to you."
Numbers 6:24, 25

Table of Contents

Acknowledgements: iii

Dedication:. v

Preface. ix

Stages: xi

Chapter One
Tobermory—Beginnings. 1

Chapter Two
Hamilton—A New Beginning! 31

Chapter Three
Toronto—New Growth 41

Chapter Four
Northern Ontario—More Lessons. 47

Chapter Five
Ottawa—"Ripeness Is All" 97

Conclusion. 115

Preface

The following lines are embarrassingly egocentric. Not only so, but no effort has been made to focus on the family. Indeed quite the contrary is intended, and perhaps in part achieved.

Furthermore, the reflections included are quite selective. Waning memory accounts for many 'blank pages' of personal history—even if these might have been of interest—and failure to pass the test of profitability screens out much else.

Perhaps the underlying intent of the following pages might be summed up as an attempt to set down in print some reflections on life as seen through the lens of one individual. If a 'spinal theme' is discovered in the work, it may be that it is there more by chance than by design. On the other hand, if somehow these lines reflect in some small way the goodness and patience and sovereign grace of Almighty God, the Father of our Lord Jesus, in His gracious dealings with fallen mankind, that would be a worthwhile outcome!

Stages:

*"Here are the stages in the journey of the Israelites
when they came out of Egypt by divisions
under the leadership of Moses and Aaron.
At the Lord's command
Moses recorded the stages in their journey."*

Numbers 33:1, 2

CHAPTER ONE
Tobermory—Beginnings

"You have a boy, Mary, and he looks just fine!" So might the nurse in the Red Cross outpost at Lion's Head, Ontario, have announced on that seventh day of March, 1927, as I made my debut on this world's stage. My mother would have traveled the thirty-three miles from Tobermory to give birth to her third son, the older two sons and a daughter separated by some fifteen years from this upstart. She would then have returned over rough gravel roads to the farm house that was to be my home for the next five or six years.

Named for the picturesque town of Tobermory on the Isle of Mull, Scotland, this village is strategically located at the tip of Ontario's Bruce Peninsula. Besides boasting a safe harbour for Great Lakes ships of whatever draught, it provides the point of departure for travelers taking the ferry to Manitoulin Island. Precipitous cliffs—remnants of the Niagara Escarpment—defy the waves of Georgian Bay on the east side of the peninsula while gently sloping sand beaches on the west are washed with Lake Huron's breakers. Numerous islands, many wooded, together with a few bare shoals, dot the waters to the north and east of the mainland.

One of my earliest memories involves Lake Huron and its breakers. I seem to remember the repetitive sound of the surf washing in on the distant beach. My recollections of lonely nights in my upstairs bedroom include the rhythmic wash of the swells as they came in on shore. We called them rollers, and somehow the term became enmeshed with the words of a song sung in the little country church we regularly attended: "When the roll is called up yonder I'll be there!" In my young mind I heard, 'when the rollers call up yonder . . .' I had entered a vast world and an infinitely vast cosmos!

The uniqueness of the Bruce was brought into sharp focus on one occasion later on following our move into the village when our normal classroom routine was interrupted one day by the appearance of a rare visitor. Mr. Wilson, a school inspector, had come to check on things in the school. We only sensed that he was a very important person to have in our grades one-to-eight classroom. He was an imposing man: tall, soft-spoken, wore glasses and had on a fine suit with a white shirt and a tie. This was unusual in Tobermory. There in that hushed classroom he informed us of the unique nature of our Peninsula, of the rare orchids on the Bruce, one of which we knew as the 'lady's slipper.' We lived in a special area! Until that time my awareness of our natural surroundings consisted mainly of ubiquitous cedars and honeycombed limestone. Mr. Wilson had no idea of the lasting impression he made on at least one student that day.

One other impression of a different kind remains fixed in memory, like an isolated fragment. This recollection relates to winter on the farm. The side-road in front of our farm-house was subject to winter storms complete with a generous supply of driven snow. It was this fortuitous blend of topography, wind and driven snow that occasionally created a sculptured mosaic of curves and shapes along the side of the road, transforming a common, country side-road into an art exhibition worthy of a heavenly Curator! As J. F. Millet is alleged to have observed, it was "a treating of the commonplace with the feeling of the sublime." That work of art made a lasting if sub-conscious impression of the beauty of form and balance on my mind.

The farm home, my home for the first five or so years of my life, dominated the fields on all sides. On the south, a lengthy driveway from the side-road divided two small fields and led up to the garage below the house. To the south-west more fields lay between the cedar swamp and the road. Beyond the swamp the buckwheat field nestled against the woods. Wild strawberries, occasional hazelnut trees and a huge rock made up the contents of an uncultivated area west of the farm home. A rare maple grove occupied a rise in the land also to the west, beyond which lay the last field. A pathway led from this field through the adjacent woods and ended eventually at the Belrose house, the home of distant relatives. The remains of Gordon, one of these relatives, lie buried somewhere in Italy, a youthful victim of the Second World War. To the right of the path one could travel down into the marsh where blueberries and cicadas abounded; to the left of the trail lay the woodlot and the home of the bear. The field east of the home contained a few stone piles and some resident groundhogs. They had very sharp teeth as I discovered when trying to reach into an opening in the rocks to lay hold of one of these furry creatures. He was simply defending his territory.

Sport was a black and white collie who looked after things on the farm. As a wandering pre-school farm lad I became part of his responsibility. The farm provided a good range of opportunity for wandering, whether in the lanes leading to the fields, the maple grove on the ridge to the north or the cedar swamp to the west.

One of the unexplored areas near our home lay beyond the maple grove. It was a large wooded acreage that provided firewood for the winter. Sporty and I didn't venture quite that far on our own; one could get lost there. It was this area that provided the setting for a memorable adventure for both of us. It happened between seasons, probably early spring, when my two uncles were cutting wood. Sporty and I decided that we would pay a visit to the workers to see how they were doing. We soon found them busy at their wood cutting. That entertainment didn't hold much interest for Sporty, and he wondered off into the bush in search of something more interesting. He soon found it!

He announced his find with excited barking, the tenor of which clearly indicated to me that he had made an unusual discovery. Nothing would do but that I should go and find him and see if perhaps he had cornered a porcupine. That would be bad news because porcupines, slow, ungainly and seemingly vulnerable, wear this armor of barbed needles that are potentially lethal. It wasn't a porcupine.

I couldn't see what it was at first. A large tree had fallen lifting the earth system around the roots and so creating a kind of cave. There was Sport barking with great gusto at the entrance to this den. He wasn't about to leave the scene on his own, and I went to him and pulled him back to be able to look into the dark opening to discover the source of the excitement. As I pulled his head back and looked inward, the nose of a black bear looked out at me! And there we met, five year old and cub, face to face!

I don't know which of us was the more startled! I do know that I said, "Sic-em, Sport!" and quit the confrontation as fast as my legs could carry me! The flight back to the uncles seemed completed in remarkably short time.

The men were skeptical when I announced that I had seen a bear. 'Some children have active imaginations.' (I happen to be acquainted with an outstanding example, born May 12, 2006!) At my insistence they picked up their axes and followed me toward the scene of battle. There we found the dog, head thrust down into the cave, still making a great tumult.

Sport was finally pulled out of the way, his face stained with blood from numerous scratches, and the uncles were able see for themselves that it was indeed a bear, a cub bear as it turned out, rudely awakened from his winter sleep. The bear was dispatched with the axes and the dog brought home from the field of battle to be healed of his wounds. The bear hide became a mat at my bedside, the scars on the underside reminding me of the battle. Those scars could also have reminded me that Sport willingly offered his very life for mine. That reality didn't dawn on me then, and it was only later in life that the concept of substitutionary sacrifice came to have personal significance in light of the Cross of Christ. There the Lord Jesus not only offered but willingly gave Himself for me!

The demise of the collie sometime later was mercifully kept from me. It wasn't kept from my father, however, who at the time was working about a hundred miles away. On his return home, he told us of this dream that he had experienced in which he clearly saw my brother Clarence take the now aged and infirm dog back to the maple grove and there end his life. That's indeed what had happened. There is a mystery about dreams that resists rational explanation.

A fine, two-story brick farm house, typical of such homes built at the end of the 19th or early 20th century, topped a prominent elevation; the landscape falling away on the south to the garage and long lane leading to the road; to the west a well-traveled path led down past the henhouse on the right and the vegetable garden to the left with its stone 'fence,' and then on to the barn and fields. The family outhouse with its complimentary Eaton's catalogue stood not far from the back door. Indoor plumbing had not yet arrived.

It was at this stone fence that one of the residents of the hen house and I amused ourselves. At least I was amused. I have no idea where the name Loki came from, but this name seemed to fit this compliant hen. At least that name survives the many decades since I played with her at the farm. Perhaps the name derived from some other source on some other occasion. Time blurs the edges and obscures the details even of the central figures of memories. The distant vista viewed from a certain point may reveal hills and even mountains in the distance but quite miss the valleys and streams between.

Loki and I 'played' by the low stone wall next to the vegetable garden just off the pathway to the barn. The wall was constructed of stones without mortar, and with a few deft maneuvers some stones could be loosened and shifted so that a space could be opened in the wall. This space became Loki's temporary residence. With a little persuasion on my part she played her role in the little drama by fitting into the cave. Why she submitted to this un-poultry-like behaviour remains something of a mystery.

Entrance to the home brought one immediately into the kitchen, a spacious room complete with hardwood floor and wainscot. A large table stood in the central space in the room. It was here that we ate all the meals, apart from Sunday dinners. These latter took place from time to time in the parlour, complete with white tablecloth and special desert—often preserved raspberries. Bread, home baked, of course—liberally spread with farm fresh butter—was required with preserved fruit so that the preserves would go farther! Well-worn maxims shaped our attitudes and guided our behaviour in those days: "Waste not want not"; "A penny saved is a penny earned"; "Willful waste brings woeful want." Even to this day these adages occasionally surface to provide contrast to the current throw-away society. Little was thrown away from that kitchen. Mother knitted warm woolen socks there by that table and repaired there as well. Little wonder that I still out of habit shut off lights not in use.

Adjacent to the kitchen was the wood shed, the storage place for fire wood for the kitchen stove. It was also the place of discipline, with assorted pieces of cedar kindling piled handy nearby. My mother would choose a piece of cedar to apply to the offender until 'atonement' was completed. Loud wailing usually preceded the event in hopes of reducing the force of the coming whacks. Such discipline was my mother's responsibility, and had it occurred in the 21st century, she might have been liable for child abuse. I don't think it did any permanent damage. Moreover, I developed affection for her that I never knew for my father.

The kitchen stove occupied a prominent position. Multiple lids; a warming closet above where mother placed wet mitts to dry; a reservoir to the right containing warm water for washing and a large oven made up this grand old farm kitchen range. (It was here that my mother caught me on one occasion on my way to the community towel to dry my hands for dinner: "Look at your wrists; get back and wash them." My response, "But I haven't dried them yet," carried little weight. This area was our washroom as well as a gathering place. Saturday night baths took place in the adjacent pantry, complete with a large copper boiler.) That oven became the source of magnificent aromas, especially on Saturdays as the week's supply of bread was prepared. White bread, brown bread, one loaf of raisin bread, and a supply of sticky-buns completed the assortment. Often we were treated to oatmeal cookies and/or gingersnaps.

Our family included my father Tom (not Thomas, and no middle name,) my mother, Mary (Ellen Bartman); their children Percy, Clarence, Eileen, a lengthy hiatus, then myself and Stanley, born handicapped in mother's later child-bearing years. Clarence, the hard-working farmer among us, inherited the farm. Percy followed our father's occupation of working with timber, whether manufacturing lumber for sale or using it in construction. His ninetieth birthday became an occasion for a gathering of a number of family members in Tobermory. On invitation from the family I gave the following genuine tribute:

PERCY: ON THE OCCASION OF YOUR NINETIETH BIRTHDAY, July 31, 1999

A little casual research has uncovered the fact that you have become a member of a somewhat exclusive club—the Nonagenarians! Your fellow-members—all in their nineties—are reaching forward to the privilege of joining the centenarians, and in so doing gaining the perks that go with that rare attainment.

One of the earliest memories I have of my brother illuminates in a remarkable way the relationship that I had with him in those early days. It involved money, and money in the depression years was scarce to say the least. I must have been about five years of age. (The depression closely followed my appearing on the scene, and I don't want to speculate on any connection between these two events!) Saturday nights were special in those days. We lived on a farm outside the village of Tobermory, and we looked forward to the end of the week when we would all wend our way with the other residents to the town's busy street. Two general stores, Belrose's and Golden's, provided for the needs of the residents of the community.

They also provided treats for children—at a price, of course! One cent would buy any one of a range of colourful offerings in large glass containers placed where we could easily see them, and five cents made one feel quite wealthy! And this is where my earliest recollections of Percy come in. He was my source of revenue. I would approach him for a hand-out, assured somehow in my innocence that I wouldn't be turned down. I wasn't disappointed. Not one cent or two, but a nickel! That wasn't a loan, by the way; it was a no-strings-attached hand-out, enough for an ice cream cone!

Another early memory relates to our younger brother, Stan. Stan was born a Mongoloid baby, and I had little patience with him, I'm embarrassed to admit, even though I was closest to him in age. He became the care of our sister Eileen when he was older, and she gave of herself unselfishly for his welfare. It was Percy, however, as I recall in those early days who entertained him with little amusements. One such entertainment Percy provided consisted of the rapid and rhythmic manipulation of his two hands on the table to the accompaniment of the rhyme, "Go to bed Tom, Go to bed Tom." I was intrigued by the thing, and Stan would erupt in gales of laughter, no matter how often it was repeated.

"I Never Did Learn to Dance"

Percy dropped out of our lives for some years when he enlisted in the Royal Canadian Engineers. The Second World War took him to England, the Mediterranean area, and then towards the end of the war to continental Europe. Building bridges in war zones may not have been the safest of wartime occupations, but it was probably less hair-raising than his task of locating and disposing of land-mines. Being courageous under adverse conditions wasn't entirely new to Percy: if you ask him, he can relate some harrowing experiences out on Georgian Bay in a small boat and a big storm.

With the end of the war came demobilization and a return to 'civy-street' with all the challenges entailed. This prompted one of the rare memories of our relationship. Percy asked me for my advice on what kind of clothing he ought to buy. Here I was, a teenager struggling to know who I was and what I should wear. It was about that time that I became the dubious owner of a so-called Sinatra jacket, all the rage among the teens in Hamilton at that time.

It was at that time too that Percy became the owner of a car, a Ford V8, I believe it was. I thought that it was neat. It had lots of power.

It was also about this time that a most significant event occurred, an event with consequences continuing to this day: he had escaped death, imprisonment or injury during those years at war, but now a talented and beautiful young lady from the city of Hamilton captured his heart. Not long after this, Audrey Jenkins became his wife and my sister-in-law, and the rest, as they say, is history! By the way, he didn't ask my advice about either the car or the bride!

The years since have been occupied with the daily round of life: working, providing for a growing family, and, one ought to add, delightful seasons hunting and fishing!

What are we to say of such a life? Each one here this evening will have his or her own thoughts, depending on one's point of view. I trust you will make wide allowance for bias as I briefly share my own observations.

Percy's was an ordinary life, one neither marked nor marred by show or swagger or ostentation. Rather, the following terms come easily to mind: modesty, reliability and constancy, qualities of character not all that abundant in our society. Even though I'll always be stuck in the junior role, I speak from the heart, Perce, when I say that I count it a privilege to be named as your brother!

In conclusion, I must make mention of one 'complaint.' You folks just knew that all this was too good to be true, didn't you? Gwen and Doug, you might be interested in some hitherto unrevealed escapade involving your father. And you grandkids, wouldn't you like to hear some wild story about grandpa? Well, I'm sorry to have to disappoint you. All that I've said is to the best of my recollection the truth. If it's not the whole truth, it's because I don't have access to that; that's God's department. No, my complaint isn't with Percy; it's with this God who knows all the truth about all of us.

My complaint is this: In my limited judgment, if access into heaven were on the basis of a life well lived, it would seem to me that this man would easily qualify for consideration. Is he perfect? Of course not. Only One fits that category, and He's the One who made this astonishing and provoking statement about those He called to live with Him in heaven: *"I have not come to call the righteous, but sinners."* I wouldn't have said that, but then I didn't love those sinners and die on the cross for them, paying their sin-debt in full.

But I'll have to be content to wait a while to take up this matter with the One responsible! Either the Lord Jesus had things topsy-turvy, or else maybe—just maybe—we need to see things as He sees them! And I think I know who has things right.

I know that others will join with me in wishing you well as you enjoy many good years in the Nonagenarian Club!

In the meantime, Percy, I know that it's not Saturday night, but we have come together in Tobermory, and I still like ice cream cones: *Do you happen to have a nickel?*

"I Never Did Learn to Dance"

"You'll be lying under Eileen's blanket," Joan said. She had just made the bed and I was heading that way. That was my sister Eileen! She was my only sister and I'm thankful that we got along well. I have few memories of her while she was still at home on the farm. One curious moment occurred on a Halloween night when this ghostly, masked figure appeared at the farm house door to ask for a treat. "M-U-M's the word; M-U-M's the word!" moaned this visitor, especially for my benefit. I finally caught on. She had a great sense of humour as well as a fiery temper to match her auburn hair. Both she and Clarence inherited this temper from our father who was known to 'blow up' one minute and be singing, quite at peace with the world, the next.

Eileen probably made some bad choices at one time or another—who of us hasn't—and the consequences stayed with her for life. To her great credit, she did not seek to escape her lot, but stayed by her husband and family. One of the unselfish and loving choices she made was to 'take in' Stan and care for him when he was too much for our mother. This unselfish care continued until Stan's death at a late age (mid-fifties?) for a person with Down's Syndrome. Eileen also knew what it was to suffer grief. Erma, a lovely daughter of nine years was walking home on the highway with a girl-friend one evening when she was struck from behind by a car and killed instantly. The friend was spared. The driver had evidently been drinking. A son Clifford, a member of the Toronto Police Force, died of natural causes in his mid-twenties.

Eileen had specified that there was to be no funeral service, no 'speaking well of the dead,' at her passing. That was like her. I was privileged to say a few words in her well-deserved honor at the graveyard at Dunk's Bay when her body was committed to the sandy soil. This was one time she didn't have the last word!

"The Harbor" was really the 'raison d'etre' for this quaint community of about five hundred souls in the nineteen-thirties. It was really two harbours, designated by the locals as Big Tub and Little Tub. The designation "Tub" derived from Tobermory, locally pronounced 'TUBm-MERy.' A rare, resident doctor had aptly coined the phrase, "Over the washboard into the Tub," in reference to the rough gravel road leading to and from civilization in the south. I have heard that in stretches where a firm foundation was lacking, this road was originally laid over a base of poles laid side-by-side. Small wonder that it achieved a wash-board effect! I routinely experienced car-sickness when traveling south over seemingly endless sharp hills.

Big Tub had the distinction of being a safe haven from stormy weather, aligned and protected as it was from 'weather' from either Georgian Bay on the east or Lake Huron on the north and west. It is unusually deep; sheer rock faces on either side of this long narrow harbour plunge straight down to unseen depths. Floating docks served to moor visiting yachts in summer. These opulent craft with their varnished planking and mahogany decks were a source of endless wonder to young village lads! They were totally unlike the rough, locally made fishing tugs docked in Little Tub. Occasionally a large pleasure craft that disdained docking with the others would anchor in mid-harbour (between the two harbours) and send a small boat in to the dock. Such a luxurious vessel became the source of admiration to those of us who ventured out in our little rowboats to gaze in youthful awe as we circled it in our little home-made craft. A sunken shipwreck at the end of Big Tub also provided endless hours of entertainment to us young dreamers in our row-boats as we gazed down through crystal clear waters at the remnants of bygone days.

Little Tub lay bordered by docks, the anchorage of fishing tugs and in summer of various visiting craft. On higher ground beyond the docks were two general stores, the post office, the barber shop, a library with a massive stone fireplace crafted by my father, and mingled with and beyond these the residences of what were mostly fishermen. Saturday night saw farm folks from the country come in on foot or by car to meet together, shop and socialize.

"I Never Did Learn to Dance"

After the building of a saw-mill, we moved to a new home in the village. The mill was strategically located on the water-front so that logs cut on Yeo Island and transported by water could be landed there. Each log was stamped on the butt end with a TS so that our father could reclaim it in event of loss in transport during one of our frequent storms. This is so like the biblical truth which affirms that God marks each believer with a special seal of ownership: God *"set his seal of ownership on us, and put his Spirit in our hearts as a deposit, guaranteeing what is to come"* (2 Corinthians 1:22). Many a tale emerged from those ventures on stormy waters, and likely will from these latter adventures as well!

This move to the village meant leaving that stone walled country school in grade one. That building is still preserved, now as a museum, the "Peninsula & St. Edmunds Township Museum," housing a variety of interesting artifacts from another era.

A narrow gravel road servicing a few scattered homes and a number of tourist cottages wended its way along the lakeshore from the village of Tobermory to where we now lived. The cottage owners would appear in late spring or early summer and disappear as fall came. Our home, about a fifteen-minute walk from the center of the village, lay on one side of the road and the waters of Tobermory Harbour on the other. Countless trips to the rocks at water's edge with two pails provided fresh clean water for our household needs. Pure drinking water was not a problem in those days.

It was here that I made acquaintance of a young crow. The Crow didn't have a name. We had become acquainted after our family moved from the farm into "The Harbour." The circumstances and details of that first introduction are lost in the dim past, but the main facts follow.

The Crow evidently—and I say evidently because I have no memory of the details—came into my acquaintance early in its fledgling life. What I do know is that by day when I was around home, he sat on my shoulder as I walked about. At night he stayed in the woodshed. I looked after his dietary needs and in return became his confidante. He made no effort to leave such an amicable relationship. Little did I realize that that friendship was to prove his undoing.

I came home one day to learn that one of the cottagers had shot The Crow. Whether that person—and I never discovered the identity of the perpetrator—found it to be a nuisance or a challenge for target practice is unknown. It was likely done in all innocence. From the present point of view, one crow more or less is of little concern. To a boy of seven or eight the loss of a carefully trained pet through entirely preventable means was heart-wrenching.

After our move we now could now gaze across the outer waters of Tobermory Harbour and on down the length of Big Tub. I then became addicted to the water, rather than to my former love of wandering the woods with the dog. Winter saw the harbour frozen over with a thick layer of ice. One of my chores was to make frequent trips down to the hole chopped through the ice to get fresh water for household use. Summer, on the other hand, gave opportunities for using the punt or later the little home-built sail boat. No doubt it also hastened the accumulation of grey hair on my mother's head when I ventured out into the Harbour and beyond to explore the islands nearby.

Living in Tobermory did not provide great opportunity for travel. We were fifty miles or so from Wiarton, the nearest town of any significance. So it was with considerable excitement that we students in grade eight looked forward to a class trip to Stratford, Ontario, to see the King and Queen!

The year was about 1939; hostilities loomed in Europe, and their Majesties took the opportunity to visit Canada, possibly with the hope of stirring up support for the 'mother-land.' Whatever the purpose of the visit, it provided a once-in-a-lifetime opportunity for some young citizens to see royalty up close—or so we hoped. That reality finally neared after an hours-long bus ride and what seemed like an hours-long wait beside the railway track in

"I Never Did Learn to Dance"

Stratford. The train carrying their Majesties was late, but we finally heard the report that that it was near.

We strained our eyes down the deserted track, hoping to get a glimpse of this royal train. Finally, there it was. Rounding the distant curve, it bore down upon us with what seemed unnecessary speed. Not only so, but it sped past us, barely decreasing its hurry, leaving us looking up the other direction at the departing caboose. Then it happened. In the shrinking dimensions of this royal express we were able to discern what appeared to be two figures emerge and wave at the crowd below. These two, we were assured, were indeed our King and Queen.

The lesson that might have been learned then (it wasn't!): Travel does not always live up to the promotion encouraging it or to the expectations of those who indulge.

This phase of my life brought me under the discipline of elementary school, up to grade eight. That discipline took concrete form on two occasions when I experienced the consequences of transgressing the Law. It mattered little that the particular ordinance I offended was unwritten. The particular regulations concerned and all the other regulations making up the cannon of that law were evidently entirely in the mind of Miss Irene MacKinnon but that didn't abate their force. I found this out one day when the class became noisier than usual and the solemn warning was issued: "No more noise—no whispering." I did not intend to challenge the Law, and I have no idea of what possessed me to ask my neighbour for an eraser. That I broke the decree discreetly mattered not. "Arnold: out into the porch." Out I marched and out came the Enforcer of the Law with the traditional strap and administered the just punishment. I survived, but I didn't brag about the incident.

The other transgression was more blameworthy. It was winter, and the snow ideal for making snowballs. Outside the classroom and on out through the porch and the entry lay the veranda. At recess it was customary for the girls to remain on the veranda while the boys engaged in snowball skirmishes. I thought that it would be a challenge to see if I could throw a snowball across the veranda without hitting any of them. I failed. The wounded student complained to the Law Enforcer and it was a case of justice not delayed. The porch, the strap and the lesson learned. Life is full of lessons, some of them serious.

There I also learned that there were these mysterious and fascinating creatures called girls. I competed for top spot in the class with two of them: Margaret Ritchie and Lorraine Ransberry. Grade eight marked the end of formal education for a while. It was also at this time that I made my first futile attempt to learn to dance with one of these strange members of the human race. I found myself years later unwillingly thrust into a situation where I was required to participate in dancing in a wasted effort to round out what was lacking in my teaching expertise. My partner must have wondered about the nature of my developmental deficiency that was responsible for such ungainly moves on the dance floor. I never did learn to dance. It is interesting but futile to speculate on what may have been the outcome had I inherited that facility and chosen "the road not taken."

The Concise Oxford Dictionary defines dance as follows: "Dance (dah-), v.i. & t. Move with rhythmical steps, glides, leaps, revolutions, gestures, etc., usu. to music, alone or with a partner or set..."

My deficiency in this particular skill has surfaced from time to time over the course of my life. One incident from my teaching years may illustrate the obvious nature of this lack.

Paul Ducharme was our school librarian. Wavy black hair mixed with touches of grey crowned his black eyebrows and rounded face and torso. Not only did he keep the library in strict order, but he also kept meticulous notes on the events of his life. These daily notes were duly transferred to a diary and then in turn to an annual log which he sent to a publisher, there to be made into a hard cover volume reflecting his life and thought for that year. He was amassing an impressive library of which he was the singular author.

"I Never Did Learn to Dance"

It was during these years while we were together at Chelmsford Valley District Composite School that Paul exercised his considerable missionary zeal in an effort to undermine my Christian faith and win me over to his agnosticism. His university experience in gaining a degree in Journalism had shattered whatever faith he had in the Catholic Church. Science became his refuge. He would often appear at the door of my classroom at the end of the school day and engage me in critical debate. I composed the following parable for him as a response that seemed to me to illustrate the disparate philosophical positions of the two of us:

> Two brothers once came to inherit an island in the tropical part of the ocean. They found the island a delightful place with forests and hills and valleys, as well as beautiful sand beaches.
>
> One significant problem soon became evident: they lacked a source of fresh water. In spite of a preliminary search of the island they located only brackish ponds whose waters, though potable, were distasteful.
>
> They determined that they would need a good source of water if they were to enjoy the other benefits of their inheritance. A disagreement arose as to how this situation could be resolved. As a consequence, the brothers each went his own way: the one trained in the sciences set out to make a geological survey of the island to determine the best possible location for a well, the other went his way, having only an old manuscript he had found, supposedly showing the location of a spring.
>
> After some time they met together to share their findings. The first brother reported finding promising areas for a supply of water. The second

brother reported excitedly that he had indeed found the spring noted in the manuscript! "It's just where it says," he said; "on a rocky outcrop with a Tree marking the place. I tasted, and it's very satisfying!"

The older brother would hear nothing of this tale. He was busy writing up his survey findings.

Scientific investigation is a remarkable tool. By this means men (and women) are able to peer into the make-up of the tiniest bit of matter or, alternatively, reach into the more distant parts of our universe.

There is, however, a practical limit to man's reach. No matter how far he is able to venture into the vastness of space with vehicles and instruments crafted on earth; no matter how much further he can 'see' beyond these travel limits with powerful astronomical telescopes, there will always be a limit beyond which only his imagination can carry him.

This limitation may be likened to a giant bubble in which is confined all material existence, all that has come into being at some time or other. Outside that theoretical bubble lies a reality completely other! It is quite outside the ken of the scientist and his instruments. We can only know it by report.

(This scenario was crudely drawn on the blackboard in Room 127 for the benefit of a certain librarian. All to no avail, of course.)

Paul had a total disregard for the conventions usually found in men. New toys such as cars are carefully guarded lest a scratch should mar their perfection. On one occasion he purchased a new car, and then proceeded to alter it to fit his perceived needs. He hand painted some parts of the car; removed the passenger seat to provide sleeping accommodations; adapted the trunk area to provide a table for lunch time. The new vehicle was now ready for his summer vacation ventures.

"I Never Did Learn to Dance"

Sometimes he and a friend would opt for motorcycles for such travel. I envied him his powerful highway bike.

He was closer to the truth than he imagined when at the end of one school day he came into Room 127 on his usual mission of undermining my Christian faith. I suspect that he would have been more comfortable in his agnosticism had I shared it with him. After the usual banter, he commented derisively, "I'll bet you couldn't even 'shake-a-leg'!" I didn't attempt to deny the accuracy of his analysis; indeed I may have taken some secret satisfaction—and perhaps some pride as well—in thinking of myself as superior to such worldly pleasures. From that early, awkward introduction to dancing there in that little ice cream parlour at the head of Little Tub harbour to this day, 'moving with rhythmical steps' has not been my forte. Paul had put his finger on an evident deficiency in my life.

It may well be significant that the first two mentions of dancing in Scripture reflect two different aspects to this activity. The first mention occurs in Exodus 15 in that triumphal celebration of the mighty deliverance Jehovah had given the Israelite survivors from Egypt. *"Miriam the prophetess, Aaron's sister, took a tambourine in her hand, and all the women followed her, with tambourines and dancing."* Even here it is notable that Moses is not included in the dancing even though he was included in the singing described in verses one and two where the glory is ascribed to the Lord.

The second mention of dancing is recorded in Chapter 32 of Exodus. Moses had stayed on the mountain with the Lord receiving instructions for the people of Israel as to how they were to live as the people of God. That stay outlasted the patience of the people who remained in the camp, and they asked Aaron to make them gods who would lead them back to Egypt. Out of this request came the golden calf and the religious revelry that Moses heard as he descended from the mountain to the camp. They had sacrificed burnt offerings and peace offerings to this idol and afterward *"sat down to eat and drink and got up to indulge in revelry."* This was the scene when Moses approached the camp and *"saw the calf and the dancing,"* evidences of a people *"running wild."* It was indeed religious, but utterly sensual, and the outcome of that revelry was death for thousands.

There is *"a time to mourn and a time to dance,"* says the writer of Ecclesiastes (3:4), and perhaps the time for dancing in appropriate freedom and motivation will come with the appearing of the kingdom of God. Until then we must cope with what the Bible calls the flesh, that innate tendency to wrong, as Herod found out to his chagrin on the occasion of his birthday party: *"On Herod's birthday the daughter of Herodias danced for them and pleased Herod so much that he promised with an oath to give her whatever she asked"* (Matthew 14:6f.). The consequence of that birthday party with its sensual dancing was that godly John the Baptist was beheaded.

The act of writing poetry is like dancing—it involves the rhythm of sounds, whether the sounds are merely within the head or are spoken. It is on a different level than mere prose. Dancing, on the other hand, necessitates the rhythm of physical movement. "True ease in writing comes from art, not chance/As those move easiest who have learn'd to dance" (Pope, 'An Essay On Criticism'). I make a clumsy attempt at poetry (and in so doing demonstrate that I am not a poet) and muse about Mephibosheth (See 2 Samuel 9) and imagine that I recognize in him a kindred spirit:

Mephibosheth Today

"Do not fear"
    You behind the dark tree
    Eyes anguished with guilt's dread and love's purpose
    Deep as Calvary's piercing
    and you behind the mask
    fashioned for the Just Society
        now playing
        panned by critics

"I Never Did Learn to Dance"

        likely to close soon
        and does anyone know what will be next
            Does ANYONE KNOW
and you with anxious mien
"Do not fear"

"I will show you kindness"
    the deed written in Golgotha's indelible love
    in letters large as Jesus here like me
    Jesus there for me
    now in whelming waves of cool fire
        along the fibers of my moments
    "I will show you kindness"

"I will restore the land"
    ragged heir of creation's scepter
        dreams of wealth once held
        dreams of wonders tomorrow
        test-tube, smoke and peace corps dreams
    the scepter has become a serpent
    you shall have dominion
    and I now challenge the lower beasts of the field
    and the higher birds of the sky
    with a scepter forged in a cruel Furnace
    and marvel at its illusion
    as I sympathize with Adam in his loss
    "I will restore . . ."

"You shall eat at my table"
    and shall I eat with You
        what does your table look like
        and what the paneled walls of bliss
        and what the serried ranks of those who serve. . .
    the table is now set in a crowded wilderness
    the rich bread is coarse and hard

       and good and acceptable and perfect
           when one is hungry
           when one is hungry it is good . . .
       I do not like the wine
       it savors of that Furnace
       it is forever tainted by that Forge
       it has become bitter
       I do not like the wine here
       "You shall eat at my table"

And shall I eat with YOU?
    "Do not fear
I will show you kindness
I will restore the scepter
and you shall eat at my table"

The dance seems a bit more orderly when I pen these lines:

On Reading of the kings of Isreal

How flawed the greatest men of earth,
How weak the wisest king;
How comforting to turn from these
To the Christ of whom we sing!

"This is my Son," blest word we hear,
How fresh it falls from heav'n;
It points us upward to throne
Where sits that Son once giv'n.

The Object of the Father's love,
He rests there without peer;
By virtue of His precious blood
We too have been brought near.

"I Never Did Learn to Dance"

"I am well pleased with Him," we read,
The Father speaks the word;
And in that Person and His work
We rest—in one accord.

Both dancing and writing poetry require the release of those controls that govern the normal manner of life in these areas. Ordinarily one moves physically or constructs units of speech mentally in a prosaic fashion. We don't normally dance while doing our daily jobs nor do we speak poetically in normal workplace conversation. To write poetry or to dance requires that one shift into that other appropriate mode—a conscious transition. It's escaping the dull, pedestrian and unromantic way of life.

A near approach to 'dancing' in a spiritual mode came during the times in Iroquois Falls, particularly in connection with fellowship with Herb Peever at Montrock Chapel. He and I could see eye-to-eye on things in the spiritual realm. We 'moved together' on a variety of elements without the intrusion of disparate goals.

The same experience came while I was at Parkside Ranch for a summer session. Then I was, as it were, on my own, doing physical work around the farm in spare time and giving myself to 'spiritual work' as opportunity opened. This latter work involved visitation, small group Bible studies and occasionally speaking formally. It was then that I had the sense of being 'carried along' in some way. It may not have been dancing, but it was toward the opposite end of the spectrum from the dull and prosaic.

It's no doubt true that I avoid certain kinds of 'spiritual dancing.' I have felt quite out of place in certain group situations, even where Christians were involved, where I sensed a psychological pressure to join in with the crowd around me, whether in clapping the hands, raising the arms, simply standing on cue from the speaker, or even swaying to the rhythm of the music. One of the more interesting discoveries on coming to Ottawa was the phenomena of 'weavers,' 'rotators' and 'bobbers'! These may be observed in large and lively congregations, responding to the rhythm of the music. The weavers sway from side to side, the rotators gyrate from right to left, while the bobbers rise on their tip-toes, all in time to the same beat. I find it difficult to relinquish control of my "prosaic pace" in order to join the dance.

I am reminded of portraits of my solemn forbearers from a bygone era that gaze down from their place of rest. No suggestion of a smile is permitted to these austere pioneers. In the Bartman home, and in my mother's home, Sundays were especially sober. No whittling was allowed, and no whistling was heard on the 'Sabbath.' Truth be known, some of these, like my aunt Pearl Robins, were known to be quite lively. Joan and I have heard her at the piano, fairly making it dance!

A song that has attained some popularity in some quarters contains the words, "'I am the Lord of the dance,' said he," suggesting that the Lord Jesus is the spirit moving folks in this activity. It has a suitably bouncy, toe-tapping rhythm calculated to get the audience into the mood. It has never been one of my favourites. The Roman author Cicero seems more fitting to my temperament: "No man who is sober dances, unless he is out of his mind, either when alone or in any decent society, for dancing is the companion of wanton conviviality, dissoluteness, and luxury."

I can't imagine the Lord dancing during His sojourn here on earth. Here He was seen as the Man of sorrows. "Forever on Thy burdened heart a weight of sorrow hung," sings Denny. No doubt Denny would agree that the word "forever" applied particularly to our Lord's earthly time in this scene. The Scriptures seem to point to an experience of victory as the occasion for dancing. Miriam led the other women with tambourines in song and dance when the Israelite nation emerged triumphant through the Sea. Jeremiah prophesies of a time yet future when that nation will again experience triumph, this one more righteous, more universal, more enduring when God's Christ will be on the throne:

"I Never Did Learn to Dance"

I will build you up again
  and you will be rebuilt, O Virgin Israel.
Again you will take up your tambourines
  and go out to dance with the joyful. (Jeremiah 31:4)

That joyous time may be very near for Israel, and if that is so for Israel, how much nearer for us. Perhaps I will have learned to dance by then.

Summers in Tobermory provided opportunity for employment and on one occasion I became a chore-boy for Mr. Lloyd Phelps, one of the annual summer visitors to the Tub. Part of my duties involved traveling in my employer's car. Two distinctive memories of that car remain to this day. Mr. Phelps owned two beautiful dogs, retrievers of some kind, and these dogs accompanied us on these little journeys. It is said that the sense of smell is the most lasting in our memories. The combination of closed windows and the reek of dogs in the warm summer days provide a lasting memory. Then, too, Mr. Phelps chewed tobacco which required him to frequently spit out the 'juice.' Normally this is not a problem, but when driving a car the spittle needs to go out the window. This is not a challenge either, except that the window should be open. A tobacco-stained driver's-side window bore witness that the window was not always open! Nevertheless this was a paying job and the money, though not plentiful, was sure.

A paper route also provided an income, a little more plentiful in theory and a little less certain in fact. I would go daily to the Belrose General Store, located on the main street of the village, to collect and sort the papers in preparation for delivery. I also "collected" some other items while in the store. Making sure no-one was watching, I regularly purloined packages of gum and candy and stowed them in my paper-bag.

Years later at a meeting in Central Gospel Hall in Toronto, a missionary from South America spoke from that delightful little letter of the apostle Paul to his friend Philemon. In his address the missionary touched briefly on the need for restitution on the part of Christians.

At this time I experienced something quite new and disturbing. I had been a Christian for about a year and was attending Bible School, but the notion of restitution had never dawned on me. Now conscience smote me! I had stolen from others and had never paid them for their loss. I therefore owed them compensation. Was the past not gone forever? Nobody knew my wrongs. Let bygones be bygones. But the Spirit of God compelled me to write a letter explaining the reason for the enclosed cheque and send it to each of those offended in this way. The cheques were never cashed, but my conscience rested.

Youth is often characterized by a certain enthusiasm that gradually moderates and becomes the carefulness of more mature years. This was illustrated shortly after I became a believer in Christ. It happened during my first year at Emmaus Bible School in Toronto (now Emmaus Bible College in Dubuque, Iowa), where I was introduced to a whole new 'universe of discourse,' utterly foreign to my first twenty or so years. My responsibility, it seemed, was plain: My first years were spent largely in Tobermory where to my knowledge the truth of the gospel was unknown. Religion was there; church-going was the custom for my mother and me as well as a few other families in town, but the simple good news of the grace of God never dawned on me. I had found this new truth and it was evident that I was obligated to share it with my unenlightened townspeople. So I planned to evangelize my home town.

It so happened that one of my teachers in Bible School, a godly, humble man named Harold Harper, so impressed me that I determined to ask him if he wouldn't come to Tobermory to preach to the folks of my home town that coming summer. It didn't dawn of me that I was being presumptuous in asking this busy visitor from the States to travel miles north to a remote village in Ontario. He graciously consented.

The gospel campaign was set. I arrived in the town early to prepare the way. I had flyers printed and delivered to each household in the village. The folks generally were patient with me. The Community Hall, largest hall in the village, was secured for the two weeks of the meetings. I eagerly awaited the coming of the speaker and the beginning of the campaign.

Opening night arrived. Mr. Harper and I arrived early to await the crowds. He played the piano while we waited—and waited—and waited! It was about five minutes to the opening hour and not a soul was there in that spacious hall! Empty seats greeted my vision from the platform! Finally my widowed cousin, Margaret Ransberry and one other lady appeared to make up our audience. The good folks of my home town didn't persecute me; they simply ignored me! I was utterly deflated. Mr. Harper was quite unperturbed. I was the one who had lessons to learn and he was still my teacher! By common agreement we held the rest of the meetings in the United Church. My cousin professed to come into the assurance of salvation during that time. I hope to see her in heaven.

On Sailing from Tobermory: May 25, 2007

The ubiquitous cedars and limestone rocks are just as attractive as ever. Even the thick undergrowth is inviting. 'If I owned one of these properties, I would clear little trails for walking.' So I dream. 'The rest would be left to nature.'

The limestone of the Bruce is evidently not limestone, but rather a similar formation with a significant difference. Its name is something like 'lobo stone.' My authority: Victor Last, a retired teacher in Wiarton who operates a B&B in a unique, vintage home replete with odds and ends inside and out from various parts of the globe. It was well worth the visit.

My roots are here in the Tub, and I'm aware of a kind of reluctance to be separated from these roots as we prepare to set sail. Something in me yearns to hang on to this pleasant Shangri-La at the tip of the Bruce. But this Shangri-La exists principally in my imagination.

I see evidence of change on every side. The quaint fishing village, a centre for the few farmers on the outskirts and location of a saw-mill, has been modernized—it's caught up with the times. (Wasn't it Spenser who delved into the nature of change versus immutability? They thought on such things then.) "I change, He changes not," we sing of the One whose designation is *the Same*. I change, and my circumstances change. That's now the constant. Part of that constant involves leaving. Life is a succession of leavings. (Did someone already make that observation?) Audrey, my sister-in-law, 'left' this scene a few days ago—for good.

And so ultimately must we all leave behind the familiar place as well as other people on the same pilgrimage: the limestone, the cedars and all else that belongs to this earthly scene. The earth itself is evidently destined to face radical change. So Shakespeare prophesies in "The Tempest":

> *Our revels now are ended. These our actors,*
> *As I foretold you, were all spirits, and*
> *Are melted into air, into thin air;*
> *And, like the baseless fabric of this vision,*
> *The cloud-capp'd towers, the gorgeous palaces,*
> *The solemn temples, the great globe itself,*
> *Yea, all which it inherit, shall dissolve,*
> *And, like this insubstantial pageant faded,*
> *Leave not a rack behind. We are such stuff*
> *As dreams are made on; and our little life*
> *Is rounded with a sleep. (PROSPERO)*

How good, then, to have other roots—roots fixed, firmly imbedded in the Rock of Ages. If this earthly scene provides gorgeous geological features, glorious botanical exhibits, what unimagined splendors await in that permanent place prepared by

"I Never Did Learn to Dance"

the Maker of heaven and earth for His beloved ones, those who are trusting in Jesus!

My own move from Tobermory came at the beginning of my teenage years. I had no idea of what lay ahead of me, what persons and events I would encounter and how they would help to determine the course of my life as I moved with my father and mother to the city of Hamilton.

CHAPTER TWO
Hamilton—A New Beginning!

It is virtually impossible to sort out all the 'permutations and combinations' that factor into a decision or an event or a move. By faith we understand that God is sovereign in his working so that in the affairs of men ultimately all things will redound to his glory. The writer of the Chronicles illustrates that truth in the case of the events surrounding Rehoboam, son of Solomon, *"this turn of events was from God"* (2 Chronicles. 10:15). God was in the thing and, though Rehoboam acted completely in free will, the king was unknowingly bringing forward the sovereign purposes of God. I have no doubt that eternity will reveal that this was the case in the following course of events, and that for good!

In this regard, it is helpful to remember that though God is sovereign in all his ways and in all His creation, that this does not mean that His 'favored ones' are guaranteed an easy ride through this life. Indeed quite the opposite may be true. We read that *"the whole creation has been groaning as in the pains of childbirth right up to the present time."* And it's still groaning now, two thousand years after this was written. Believers are subject to the same storms, earthquakes, plane crashes as are non-believers, albeit only to the extent that our sovereign God allows. Christ's missionary, Paul the apostle, experienced the fury of the "northeaster" that swooped down on their ship on the tempestuous Mediterranean Sea, eventually wrecking it on the sand-bars of Malta. However, Paul and all the others with him were saved through the ordeal. God had a purpose for him still.

The decision to move from Tobermory to Hamilton included several elements: lack of employment for my father in Tobermory; employment opportunities in Hamilton in the early forties when World War Two was creating a stir; and so the lumber mill, our livelihood, was sold. There followed a temporary move into the central part of the village while my father went to look for job opportunities. The major move south to the city of Hamilton followed.

Overshadowing all was the unseen, unfelt, but very real presence of God in the outworking of His sovereign purposes in the life of a young lad on the verge of his teen years. Organized religion in Tobermory at that time consisted of one denomination: the United Church. The Roman Catholic Church had a building there, but no active members. So it was that no evangelical witness existed in the Tub at that time. I was destined to encounter new and very different information about heaven and how to get there.

The move from Tobermory to Hamilton took place without incident. My father built our new home, and that construction project occasioned one of the rare acknowledgements of the spiritual aspect of my father's life. He was not one to waste time, and on one occasion he was busy working on the building of the house on a Sunday when a photographer from the Hamilton Spectator happened along and took a picture of him working on the rafters. It was an embarrassment to him to have this published for the entire city to see that he had been working on Sunday! My mother, the spiritual light in the family, was still with us then.

That home was in the east end of Hamilton—a few blocks from a small airport and, more significantly, just around the corner from a Christian family—the Cushnies: (Coincidence again?!) godly Mr. and Mrs. Cushnie; George, Alex, Florence, Jimmy and Kenny. George was about my age, and we encountered each other on the bus to and from the central part of the city. Our common

"I Never Did Learn to Dance"

interests included the raising of rabbits, a commercial venture since these were sold to the local hospital; and the establishment of a pigeon loft, this strictly for interest in these fascinating creatures! The mystery of how they are able to return unerringly to their loft after being driven miles away and then released remains to this day. It seems to me that those who promote evolution as the answer to these mysteries have a great challenge here.

George Cushnie senior was my first glimpse of saintliness in human form (apart from my mother) that I can recall. It seemed to me that even his face 'shone' with a reflection of heaven's light! He and his wife were from the border area of England and Scotland, he from the Scottish side, she from the English. She made an excellent cup of tea, milk first, and always served in fine china.

Mr. Cushnie—and I always knew him as that—never, as far as I was aware, did anything worthy of public notice. He would not have been well known in the community at large, though his testimony at the Caroline Street Mission where the family once attended would have been bright and clear. He was an ordinary man. But that ordinary life was conspicuous by its integrity and practical holiness. He walked with a slight limp during the time that I knew him. Like Job in the Old Testament and Cornelius in the New Testament, it could, in my opinion, be said of him that he was a blameless man.

It was about this time that I entered the world of employment. I had only completed grade eight, but for whatever reasons, my father didn't see fit to arrange for my entry into high school after we arrived in Hamilton. Perhaps the fact that he had quit school around age fourteen figured into the equation; perhaps he was just too preoccupied with providing for us all in our new environment. In any case, I went to work. It must have been an ongoing concern to him, because years later when he was retired and we had a family of our own, he gave me "some money for the education of the boys"! It wasn't much, but I appreciated the token.

My first job was at Moodie Knitting Mills, operating latch-knitting machines; a brief session at the Hamilton Coke Ovens came soon after, a most disagreeable job, working graveyard shift moving a rail car along by hand using a jack device as the car was being loaded with hot, dusty coke; then came a lengthier stay at Tuckets Tobacco Co. in the shipping department. Part of the compensation here was a weekly sample of the product. A brief experimentation with various elements of the Company's products didn't 'take,' a result for which I am indebted to God's mercy. Here I encountered Jimmy, the elevator operator and crystal ball gazer. He invited me to his home for a demonstration of his skills at "a reading." There he brought out the ball carefully enfolded in a richly colored wrap and placed it on the table in front of him. I have no memory of what he saw in the depths of the crystal that evening, and I suspect that I was a poor prospect for future meetings and possible supplement to his income. I never went there again.

The demands of war opened the opportunity to acquire a skill that appealed to me. Draftsmen were needed, and an intensive night school course was offered to meet this need. (At that time my unannounced goal in life was to become an architect and this seemed akin to that.) The instructor suggested that I should have some practical experience in a machine shop in order to have firsthand knowledge of the work involved in mechanical drafting. The Steel Company of Canada had an opening for a machinist apprentice, and that's where I spent the next four years.

These four years embrace a significant turning-point in the course of my life. Employed as a machine shop apprentice, I learned the various skills of the trade, from sweeping the shop floor (my introduction to the trade!) to producing fairly complex machine parts. It was here that I encountered Everett Coles, my first example of a Christian in the workplace. He quietly lived his faith and impressed me as a young apprentice, even though neither of us may have realized it at the time.

"I Never Did Learn to Dance"

The '42 Harley, a second hand army bike, became my transportation during this time. It carried me to work five days a week; it took me downtown on Saturdays when I spent my time going to one theatre after another in what I now recognize as a futile attempt to find something satisfying in my daily round of life. Blaise Pascal is credited with the observation that we are made with a God-shaped vacuum within us that only He can fill. I could have provided living evidence to support his theory.

It was during this period that the Harley ended up in the scrap yard one morning and I ended up in the hospital with a compound fracture of the right tibia. It was a kind of irony that my mother was in the same hospital as well—facing the ultimate consequences of leukemia. I limped to her room on my new crutches. A number of uncharacteristically solemn uncles arrived there as well, an omen of imminent loss to us all. The end came soon. "I want to go home," my mother had whispered. Did "home" mean Glasgow Avenue, or heaven? In any case, I have no doubt that heaven was her destination that day.

Certainty of one's situation in the afterlife was not a strong feature in the catalogue of United Church offerings in my experience. The worshiper was urged to "do the best you can" in hope that that best would suffice before the bar of Heaven. Conscience bore witness to failure, so that certainty was never achieved. Such a hope was wavering at best. Neither God's holiness nor His grace, both of which are so crucially significant in view of the gospel and eternity, is emphasized in this system of belief. That holiness is such that all that is less than the glory of God, anything short of God's perfect righteousness, is uncompromisingly shut out of God's presence. *"Your eyes are too pure to look on evil; You cannot tolerate wrong"* (Habakkuk 1:13). On the other hand, His grace is such that *"to the man who does not work but trusts God who justifies the wicked, his faith is credited as righteousness"* (Romans 4:5). Both these concepts are foreign to the natural man, apart from enlightenment by the Spirit of God. Though reared in the Church, one might say, I was utterly blind to these significant biblical truths.

It's curious that I had neither tears nor weeping at my mother's death nor at her funeral. Rather I experienced a kind of inner numbness. It was only afterward, when I wakened in the middle of the night to reflect on my loss and consequent emptiness, together with the prospect of a more impoverished life from then on, that grieving set in and the tears came.

The Delta Tabernacle, of the Christian and Missionary Alliance (C.M.A.) persuasion, was pastored by Ernie Bailey at this time. I have nothing but good memories of this pastor. On one occasion Mr. Bailey arranged to have Dr. Hunter, C.M.A. Evangelist and Teacher, come for a series of special meetings. I was then attending the church along with the Cushnie family.

At the conclusion of one memorable meeting I was standing beside Mr. Cushnie during the singing of the closing hymn. The song-leader took advantage of the pauses between stanzas of the hymn to issue an "invitation" to any interested and exercised attendees to "come forward" for further counseling. This should have been my signal to "go forward," but I was neither interested nor exercised. My only concern was to escape this threatening atmosphere. There followed a revealing sequence of events that I could wish expunged from the record, but it's there!

(Robert Surgenor records the following little episode: "William Wilberforce and William Pitt, one time Prime Minister of Great Britain, were brilliant men. Wilberforce was concerned about Pitt's soul, and persuaded him to go with him to hear Richard Cecil, a great gospel preacher. Cecil preached a powerful message and Wilberforce was enthusiastic. Leaving the building Pitt remarked, 'I have not the slightest idea what that man has been talking about.'" My early experience exactly at Delta Tabernacle! Only the Lord can open the eyes of the blind!)

At the first invitation Mr. Cushnie who was standing beside me leaned over to ask if I wouldn't like to go forward. I had no notion of going forward, and I stalled for time, attending closely to the open hymn-book. The second invitation came with an encouragement: "You'll never regret going forward." More stalling, mumbling. The third pause came with a further incentive: "It's the best thing you can do." I still hung back, playing for time. A final opportunity came before the last stanza and with a persuasive inducement: "I'll go down with you." My resistance to the persistent encouragements of this godly man was finally exhausted. I agreed, and down we went, the well-meaning mentor and the reluctant seeker.

The final blow to any remaining hope I may have had of an early escape came with my being abandoned at the door of the counseling room: Mr. Cushnie delivered his charge into the hands of some waiting counselors and disappeared. That time in the counseling room that evening remains a blur at best. My subconscious and ultimate strategy was to escape—out of that room—out of the church—out into the liberty of the night air. My immediate response was to conform to the drill as best I knew how. I'm fairly sure this involved kneeling with others. Whether or not any word escaped my tongue I truly don't recall. The rest of the moments in that room are indistinct. I suspect that the counselors were as perplexed as I was as to why this seeker ended up in their care.

A more dangerous and incriminating trap awaited my exit from the room. It was a case of 'out of the frying pan . . .'! While most of the audience had dispersed, a number of folks remained near the counseling room door to greet those who had responded to the call and had 'gone forward.' It was obvious to them that I was one of these. I was joyously greeted, and we shook hands all around. They smile, assuming the best. I smile, and with alarming dexterity assume the role of a new believer. I then began an interlude in my life that I would love to erase: three and a half years of pretense; years of living a double life. For to some—especially those at work—I was the same as ever. To those connected with the church, I was a believer. In fact I was a fraud and a hypocrite.

To appreciate my predicament at that moment, it will be helpful to revisit my religious background. That came almost entirely from my mother's influence. She was of Methodist stock, though in my childhood she found it necessary to associate exclusively with the United Church, a bland amalgam of the Methodist and Presbyterian Churches. It was she, Methodist at heart as she remained, who took me morning, afternoon and evening to Sunday church services. My father largely ignored religion in general or tolerated it at best. Here it was under this insipid teaching, as it seems in retrospect, that I learned that God is a decent, loving sort, that he sent his Son to deal with things that are wrong, and that if only we do our best we'll be fine, and furthermore if everyone lives this way the world will get better. It's hard to gainsay such a hopeful philosophy.

So it was that in the late 1940's in the city of Hamilton I lived as a troubled teenager, boarding in the home of Mrs. Winifred Edmunds, a godly widow from the Delta. A gift from her, a little New Testament, remains in my possession to this day. I was troubled by a number of things: though a professing believer and a church attendee and living an outwardly decent life, I was inwardly empty and living the life of a hypocrite. I'd been living this way for three and a half years, and during this time I'd been noticing a godly man in the congregation named Bill Rushton, a man who seemed to me to have a radiant face. When the time came that God was to lovingly draw me to himself, I found myself sitting beside Bill at the end of a gospel meeting. When he turned, smiled and asked, "How is it with your soul?" I confessed my deep inner need. After prayer and godly counsel by a number of believers, I returned to my lodgings, knelt by my bed and called on the Name of the Lord. My actual words that night were something like, "God, make me a good Christian." I don't suggest that others use this 'formula' in an initial approach to the heavenly Father, but it may be seen to have some wisp of legitimacy in light of Jesus' record of the "lost son" (Luke 15): *"...make me like one of your hired men"*!

"I Never Did Learn to Dance"

Something happened that night, a genuine sea change in my life. The reader may find the following three-fold evidence of this change merely the consequence of subjective reasoning or wishful thinking and therefore unreliable and unconvincing, but it was real to me then and remains so to this day. First, I experienced an inner peace, a peace that extended even to my environment; I was at peace not only with God but also with God's world. Second, the Scriptures now became appealing and satisfying to me, whereas before they were obscure and puzzling. Third, I now enjoyed a happy fellowship, a genial sharing together of common interests, with other Christians. In retrospect, these benefits are neither insignificant nor without value. Not only so, but rather than diminish in value, these virtues have become more precious as they age.

It was about this time that I was introduced to a group of men from different churches who met on Thursday evenings to encourage one another in the Christian walk. These gatherings in the home of one of the men involved some Bible study, prayers, and preparations to venture out—usually on week-ends—to take meetings at Missions, senior's residences etc. At these outings, we were given opportunity to sing, to give a testimony as to how we became believers or to give a short exposition of some passage from the Scriptures.

It was at one of these ventures that I was designated to give my thoughts on a Scripture of my choosing. I was quite confident that John 3:16 would be a safe and effective text for my address. The cue was given and I got up to speak. The folks in the audience must have wondered where I had been in my discourse, where I was and where I was going. I certainly didn't know, and my chagrin after the ordeal was such that I never used that text by itself again! Life's lessons come in various classrooms.

It was also during my time with these men that I decided that I would be a missionary. Some of the men attending the Thursday evening meetings had missionary interests. In my reckoning, it seemed that to be a missionary in a foreign country was without doubt the most exalted career to which one could aspire. Therefore I purposed to pursue that goal. Then the realization dawned on me that if I were to travel half way around the world to teach God's Word, it would be prudent first to get to know what was in the Bible.

    The men of the fellowship were helpful, various ones suggesting this or that institution that provided just such training. George Cooper suggested Emmaus Bible School in Toronto, and it turned out that it provided the highest percentage of Bible course content of all. I applied for admission and was accepted and so began a new phase in my new life.

CHAPTER THREE
Toronto–New Growth

Toronto provided an entirely new perspective on life. Actually this new phase in my life began in Hamilton where God's loving and gracious sovereignty finally drew me into the embrace of this eternal relationship, a union made possible through Christ's work on the cross. From heaven's point of view, this process could in all probability be traced back to a time before birth! It was so in the case of Jeremiah and of Saul of Tarsus. *"Oh, the depth of the riches of the wisdom and knowledge of God!"* In any case, the outworking of God's sovereign purposes in my life reached this particular stage with my coming to Toronto.

The second floor of the home of Mr. and Mrs. Stan and Marie Caston and their two daughters, 1045 Logan Avenue, Toronto, became my lodging place. Doug Bramer, another young student at Emmaus Bible School, a senior, from the Oakville area was my room-mate. He had seniority rights to the bottom bunk and so I ended up in an unaccustomed role in the top. The hazards of 'living high' came sharply into focus in the dark of one night when I found myself on the floor wandering where I was and how I got there! No bones were broken, and there was nothing for it but to climb back up and get back to sleep.

Another nocturnal event of a different nature occurred during this same period. The expression, *"The Word of the Lord came to . . ."*

is found a number of times in the Old Testament. This introduction is followed by some communication from the Lord to the individual involved, usually a prophet. I am 'neither a prophet nor the son of a prophet,' but a very distinct memory of the expression, *"O give thanks unto the Lord, for He is good; his love endures forever,"* came to me during one memorable night. I had no recollection of having read this verse of Scripture—for that it is—though I must have read it at some point, having read through the Bible in the previous year.

The Caston home frequently became the gathering place for what seemed to me ladies of some standing in society. I was not at that time separated that far from a rather homespun environment on the farm on the tip of the Bruce Peninsula and in the village of Tobermory. Snippets of conversation floating up from the living room to my desk reflected an elegance and refinement quite foreign to the boy from the farm. It was at this time that another fragment from the Scriptures provided encouragement: *"Christ, in whom are hidden all the treasures of wisdom and knowledge."* I was beginning to realize that now as a Christian I had all I needed. I was thankful and content with my lot.

Conscience, that 'inborn sense of right and wrong,' faithfully discharged its duty during one experience in Toronto. I had been trained by my mother to avoid alcoholic beverages. It was part of her Methodist background and she faithfully passed it on to me. It happened at a meeting known by Christians as the Breaking of Bread. It was my first experience of a religious meeting of this sort, and I went with a few other students from Emmaus to 'break bread.' Breaking from the loaf and eating a portion of the bread was not a problem. What followed was. The partaking of the bread was followed by the passing of a chalice from person to person. I saw that each one drank from it. The cup came to me and I drank. It turned out to be my first taste of wine and came with a strong a twinge of conscience. Mother had done her job well. I got over it.

"I Never Did Learn to Dance"

During this time at Emmaus I was introduced to a whole new way of seeing my life in relation to my environment. Up until this time my world consisted of my family and a few friends. Now a whole universe of discourse opened up. The previously unknown Scriptures presented a vast, unexplored territory. One year became three. There at Emmaus I encountered godly, biblically knowledgeable giants in the Scriptures who gently led the way through these rich treasures.

Believer's Baptism as a rite in the Christian church was a new concept to me. My baptism as a professed Christian had consisted of having water sprinkled on my head when I was but an infant. The reality was that I believed nothing that was involved in the rite. Now I was faced with the truth that having placed my faith in Christ, believing that He died in my place and that in God's reckoning I had died with Christ, was buried and had risen with Him, I should now publicly demonstrate my faith by being immersed in water. This I did at Gilead Bible Chapel, Wally Deans officiating.

It was also during my stay in Toronto that I watched in some dismay as my slim bank balance grew smaller and smaller. I needed to learn an elementary and practical lesson in God's ability to meet my daily needs. And learn I did. Anxious days and meager meals lasted until finally the bank account was exhausted. Then a startling change took place: I stopped being anxious about money. It was no longer diminishing; it was gone! I found that God supplied funds for my daily needs through various means. Previously it had been like trying to swim with my feet on solid ground. It was only when I ventured into the deep water of trust was I able to experience God's supply.

This significant lesson of trust was reinforced through an event in Iroquois Falls, the circumstances of which cannot, I am convinced, be ascribed to mere coincidence. At the time I was living with Chester and Marion Donaldson in Matheson. It fell to me to travel with Chester's car each Thursday after lunch to Iroquois Falls, about a half hour away from Matheson. The afternoon was spent visiting and the evening in conducting the Bible study and prayer meeting. It was customary during these visits to be invited for the evening meal at one of the homes of the Christians. At this time I noticed the gas gage was alarmingly low, too low for a safe return to Matheson at night. My resources at the time consisted of less than one dollar, enough for a sandwich at a local restaurant, trusting God to supply. Alternatively I could use my change for a bit of fuel and skip lunch. I opted for lunch. I forgot about my predicament during the meeting that followed and, having said their good-byes, the folks began their homeward journey and I got into the car to leave. It was at this point that an unusual incident, a singular event, took place. One of the women, Daisy Bremner, had been on her way home but turned back toward me as I sat in the car preparing to leave. I rolled down the window and she handed me a two-dollar bill (there were such things then!) and said, "The Lord wants me to give this to you." Never before and never afterward did anything of this nature occur in Iroquois Falls. Coincidence? I think not!

An incident in Nigeria recorded elsewhere has remarkably similar components.

It was in Toronto that I experienced a brief stint in the shipping room at Mitchell Books, owned and operated by Gordon Mitchell. Tommy Galt taught me the skills of packing books and plaques and other materials for safe shipment across Canada. Mr. A.A. Payne who managed the store taught me how to completely relax after lunch: Stretch out on anything flat, holding a pencil in your hand. When the pencil drops you've had a rest. It works!

On one occasion the owner of the store asked me to go out and visit some of the client businesses in Toronto and show them the latest offerings. I suspect that he hoped that I might show some potential as a sales representative for the firm. Donning my only suit and a shirt and tie, I ventured out. It was a case of Saul's armor; it wasn't a fit! I wasn't comfortable in the role of salesperson. I should have learned the lesson, but I didn't. Years later I

"I Never Did Learn to Dance"

was persuaded to become a representative of a fine life insurance company and spent some years in a situation not suitable to my personality. A series of interest tests indicated that persuasiveness was far from my forte.

My address then was 12 Rose Avenue, the home of an older Newfoundland couple, John and Mary ("My little trout," as John was wont to refer to his wife), Mary's sister Elizabeth, an elderly spinster, and Miss Coombs, a deaconess at the Pentecostal church they all attended. Elizabeth was persistently burdened with the nagging uncertainty as to whether or not she had unplugged the iron, and would necessarily have to descend from her third floor room to the basement to check. "I know I unplugged it but I just had to make sure." This lady had the unusual custom of eating eggs raw.

Evening meal was provided at 12 Rose, one memory of which suffices to this day to suppress any appetite I might have for ground pork. From time to time—perhaps once a week—Mary would serve up hamburger fairly swimming in fat with little else to flavor it. I did my best to eat my share. Mealtime was often marked by John's gentle nudge: "Mary, the tea is hot." In fact it would be boiling. Meal ended, we would all kneel by our various chairs for prayers, a custom reflecting a godliness, however imperfect, experienced only in the home of this unaffected Newfoundland couple. I'll see them in heaven!

Missionary work remained, if not at the forefront, still a possible direction for my life. To further pursue the possibility of this vocation, I attended a Summer Institute of Linguistics with Wycliffe Bible Translators in Caronport, Saskatchewan. The outcome of those two months study, interesting and challenging though it was, did not indicate a clear direction for life and I returned to Toronto.

A godly elder recommended that I spend some time in Northern Ontario helping in the work of the Lord under the mentorship of Chester Donaldson, a full time worker. I followed this counsel, and so began a new phase in my spiritual journey. I packed up my few books in a homemade travel case cum 'library,' my wool blanket and a few other personal items and headed north. The elder's advice proved profitable, and a sojourn in Northern Ontario, some reflections of which are recorded below, embraced the major portion of my life.

    I was still learning!

CHAPTER FOUR
Northern Ontario–More Lessons

The summer of training in linguistics at Wycliffe, like the four years machinist apprenticeship, was packed away like out-of-season clothing or my kit of machinist tools previously, no longer the focus of activity. And so it was that I moved with my meager possessions—a few books including a Concise Oxford Dictionary and a Strong's Exhaustive Concordance, both still in use, and a wool blanket—to the home of Chester and Marion Donaldson in Matheson, a town a little east of Timmins on Highway 11.

It was during this time that I made the acquaintance of a person of note who lived the area. He was like a rare diamond that a prospector might discover, albeit a diamond in the rough, as the saying runs. Herb Peever was one of a family of twelve consisting of eleven boys and one girl that settled in and around Iroquois Falls. Thoroughly at home in the northern woods or in a canoe on water, Herb enjoyed nothing more in the out-of-doors than gathering a few sticks, starting a little fire, putting on the honey-pail to boil water for tea. Tea leaves would be tossed in loosely with the aroma soon wafting about. Tins cups filled, it was time to sit and 'yarn' or just simply to enjoy God's creation.

In spite of an ongoing concern about a latent heart condition—several of his family had already succumbed to the disease—he maintained a rigorous lifestyle. I still recall him running over rough ground with a canoe balanced on his shoulders, across a log jam on a creek, then on to the nearby lake to check on availability of fish. I carried our lunch.

Herb was the pillar of the little Christian assembly there in the area, continuing steadfastly even when few others came to his side to help. It was my privilege to meet with him and the others of the "little flock" over an all-to-brief stretch of time before I moved south to the Sudbury area. His consistent gentleness, godliness, humbleness and faithfulness to his Saviour-God endured in spite of these circumstances and in the midst of a marriage that was not all that compatible.

It is not unexpected that a rough woodsman from the Northern reaches of Ontario should have little formal education. That was Herb. (Was it grade six?) Consider my surprise when on one occasion he should invite discussion on a book he was then reading: Earth's Earliest Ages by G. H. Pember! He read and pondered concepts beyond the reach of the average experience of his contemporaries. The following is an excerpt from a letter written to me some years after my time with him in Iroquois Falls:

> "...today is one of them perfect winter days. about 4" of snow fell last night and with the sun shining brightly at a considerable slant, I thought it the prittest thing I'd ever saw, this was as I walked or rather snowshoed out to look at my B, tralps, every tree decorated to perfection, each in itself a work of art beyond human ability to duplicate. Then the silence, as I walked slowly along I became aware of the dignity of that silence which in itself is a loud clear anthem of praise to gracious benevolent & loving God."

Herb was ushered into the awesome presence of that God while out on his trap line on another occasion. He was unique, a trophy of God's grace!

"I Never Did Learn to Dance"

  In an unspoken and remarkable way, he and I enjoyed a rare fellowship, not just in spiritual things, but in general. He was like a beloved older brother to me. Here in his company I was not an interloper. We were equals, though I looked up to him. We were comfortable together. I well remember his evident anguish of heart when I told him of my decision to move away. I look forward to meeting him again in glory.

  This spirit that marked him permeated the meetings of the little assembly that met in a simple wooden structure in Montrock. Accommodations for visiting preachers were provided in an extension at the rear of the building. You could count on about six folks showing up. Ten would be a crowd, though there was room for more. A song, a reading of Scripture, an offering of praise and thanksgiving, all without haste or pressure; all these marked the meeting of that little flock. In that rare fellowship there was no need for artificial constructs, no need for histrionic performance. Dancing expertise was not a requirement.

  About this time, it was my privilege to attend a conference in the northern United States where Ben Tuininga was one of the main speakers. Little did I know that out of this conference was to come an indicator that marked a turning point in my Christian journey. The details of the event are lost, but one of his addresses contained an arrow that translated in my inmost being into a clear direction: *Prepare to take up the work of an elder.* Taking this as from the Lord, the direction in my life was set on a new course. (I met up with him in recent years and told him of his role in my life.) Marriage and family, a desirable part of the equipment of an elder, were now in view. It therefore followed that I should acquire some marketable skill in order to earn a living in order to support a family. Therefore the need for education became apparent (grade eight would scarcely count for much in the world of employment even at that time) and therefore the need for funds to upgrade. So it was that the mines in Sudbury came into view. Here a man with a grade eight education and a strong back could earn $1.96 per hour.

Somehow contact was made with Mr. Gordon Tulloch in Levack, half an hour from Sudbury and the location of a booming nickel mine, regarding the possibility of employment in the local mine. He held a responsible position in the mine. He also was the father of the little assembly in Larchwood (later renamed Dowling) where I would find Christian fellowship. It just so happened that Laurentian University was then in the process of being established in Sudbury, a melding of three faith groups, each retaining its identity: United, Anglican and Catholic. A secular element was also included in the mix. The fellowship was there, the means of earning money for upgrading my education was present and the place for this purpose was in the process of being established. A bus ride to the Sudbury area followed. More than half a century later I was still there.

(It was intended that I should be the youth leader, though I didn't know it at the time. 'I never did learn to dance.')

My first contact in the Sudbury area was with the Tulloch sisters, Donna and Joan, daughters of Gordon and Verna Tulloch of Levack, sisters of Darwin and Andrew. I waited at their apartment for a pre-arranged ride to Levack. I did not realize at the time that Joan, the younger of the two daughters, was, by the goodness and grace of God to become my wife and life-long partner and the mother of our three sons. The rest, as they say, is history.

One enduring image from this history reflecting the development of this relationship remains impressed on my memory. The setting was the church meeting. From time to time the congregation would be treated to special music during the preliminary part of the service. This special music often involved Joan and her sister Donna, the two of them performing a duet, their voices blending naturally and beautifully. I can still see Joan: tall and slender, gorgeous dark hair and alluring eyes! I was captivated! She's still—after over a half a century—tall and slender; still has dark hair, now mixed with the odd thread of grey; and still has fascinating eyes. I'm still enthralled, though the passion of youth (and I use the term youth loosely since I was about thirty at the time) has matured into the steadfast commitment of tender care! We now lean on each other—literally—as we walk on together toward the horizon.

Sid (Selvin) Rafuse, soon appeared and provided my transportation in his Volkswagen Beetle over a winding road from Sudbury to Levack. He became a close acquaintance, a consistent brother in the Lord and neighbour ever since. We were about the same age. Sid was a Nova Scotian complete with accent, and like me, lured to Sudbury to work in the mines. He and his wife Jeanie were helped much spiritually by the Tullochs and became trophies of God's grace. When was he 'born again'? He's not sure; God knows. He was of Lutheran background, and had known his share of rough early years. He was substantially illiterate but persisted with great resolve to read the Scriptures. The Bible on tapes was of great benefit to him in this regard. He was introduced to a 'second blessing' by a single lady of our acquaintance and moved with his wife from the Chapel to the charismatic groups—there to remain to the day of his death. He was still a bright witness for Christ to the end. It was my privilege to speak well of his godly perseverance at his funeral.

So it was that I became a miner. Here I learned to trust my life to those slim cables from which the cage was suspended, tightly packed full of men in mining gear. Lunch buckets were gripped between the legs to make more room for men. The exercise of trust, the obedience of faith, was required to step off the firm concrete floor and into this device that *"dangles and sways,"* as Job had observed many centuries ago when speaking of mining in his day (Job 28), though modern engineering has tamed the freedom of this cage on its present lengthy leash. This act of faith is a kind of metaphor for the spiritual realm. Both acts are predicated on the intellectual assurance of the reliability of information given concerning the safety of the venture: the strength of the cables on the one hand and the power of Christ and the efficacy of His finished work on the cross to satisfy the righteous requirements of God's holy law on the other. Faith—simple trust—works in both cases. In both cases, however, it does require that one take a step of faith: off the concrete and into the cage in the one, and off the trust of self and into the rest of trusting God in the other.

The congregation at LBC was formed and grew after a patriarchal model with both the benefits and shortcomings inherent in this form of church structure. A family atmosphere pervaded its gatherings. Here the highly respected father figure presides. Such an atmosphere provides a measure of recognition of the familiar and therefore comfort to the members. It's not a formal religious organization that may have been familiar to many of them in the past. Rather they recognized, however subconsciously, the family structure including order and godly care, security and steadiness. Such may have been somewhat absent in their own backgrounds but now seen as right. The godly father in the Christian family provides such an atmosphere. The apostle Paul was a father to the Thessalonian believers as he points out in 1 Thessalonians 2:11: *"For you know that we dealt with each of you as a father deals with his own children, encouraging, comforting and urging you to live lives worthy of God, who calls you into his kingdom and glory."* Though the patriarchal model seems to have good precedent, it might be argued that Paul's role as a father figure pertained more to the believers individually rather than to the steady state of the assembly as a whole. Then too there has been no one to measure up to the apostle since. His initial visit to Thessalonica was but three weeks or so.

A possible weakness in the patriarchal form of church government might lie in the very strength of the patriarch in his godly care for the church family: he would not hesitate to spend and be spent for the flock. They in turn would naturally be only too glad to have it so—to be content, even eager, to hear regularly from the one who loved and cared for them. The body aspect of the church on earth with the Head in heaven together with the resultant need for the members to minister to each other may not be emphasized in biblical proportions in such a model.

Since my introduction to the "assemblies" I had been taught—and still believe—that the democratic model where all members have equal say in the governing of the assembly, and the autocratic model where one man, like Diotrephes, 3 John 9, has absolute rule were both alike unscriptural, and that a wise and godly oligarchy, an assembly ruled by a few godly elders, was more in line with God's Word. This is not to say that the institution of such an oligarchy will be without problems or, on the other hand, that the patriarchal rule of the assembly is necessarily wrong. The very fact that either is composed of men guarantees the possibility—more likely the probability—of weakness and failure. Furthermore, the godly patriarch need not be one like Diotrephes who *"loves to be first."* Father figures are needed in the body of Christ. John writes of himself as a father: *"I have no greater joy than to hear that my children are walking in the truth"* (3 John 4, cf. 1 John 2:1). What an intimate and precious relationship between believers surely existed in that first century!

In retrospect, it seems almost inevitable from a human point of view that tensions between these two disparate philosophies should emerge. I was an interloper in this relatively newly established church structure and furthermore found myself unable or unwilling to "learn to dance" as the other believers evidently had. The frustrated outburst, "You run the assembly!" surely had good cause. I didn't fit in as I should have and must have caused much grief. Running the assembly was quite out of the picture for me, searching—perhaps subconsciously—for the wise oligarchy. This tendency to seek the ideal has no doubt occupied too great a part of my life.

This situation was exacerbated when I became the son-in-law of the patriarch. In retrospect it might have turned out an easier road had I recognized the fundamental lack of being *"like-minded"* (Philippians 2) and moved on. Strangely, that possibility didn't occur to me at the time. It did crop up later when we as a family considered the advantages of moving to the Meaford area. Those advantages included escaping the uneasy yoke at Larchwood Bible Chapel on the one hand and embracing the freedom of an attractive life by the waters of Georgian Bay on the other. Something from my roots at Tobermory by the water still called, though subconsciously. I was convinced that both these motivations were of human origin and therefore we ignored them and stayed.

And so it was that we built a modest house in Dowling, a building later enlarged to accommodate a growing family and that provided a home for about half a century. In due time Joan and I became the parents of three sons: John Thomas, named after his father and paternal grandfather; Peter Gordon, named after his maternal grandfather (and a distant cousin whose body lies buried in a military cemetery somewhere in Italy); and David James, with no attributions—we liked the names.

John was marked, even in infancy, with an insatiable curiosity about his environment, a curiosity that occupied his extraordinarily long wake time out of his twenty-four hour day. I recall carrying him from one object to another, whether paintings or shelves on the walls. He seemed fascinated by each in turn. He hasn't changed.

Pete manifested an unusually tender heart: as a child sitting beside his mom in the meeting of the church, he would occasionally weep during the singing of hymns. One memorable incident in my experience suggests strongly that he comes by that sensitivity honestly. I was once watching a British 'whodunit' featuring a superintendent of detectives (or some such title) as the central character. This must have been the final episode in the series because the writers had the protagonist die evidently of a heart attack while alone in a park-like area. This in itself was not so moving, but what made the scene so affecting to me was the music chosen to accompany the scene. I have no idea of the identification of the piece, but I know that it had in it a quality that excited

"I Never Did Learn to Dance"

both pity and an overwhelming sense of sadness in the depths of my being. I still ponder the relationship between the harmonics of certain music or musical instruments and that other incredibly complex entity, the human spirit.

In due time, after a career in cycling that took him to many countries around the world, David met and married a beautiful, talented and godly young lady from Ottawa: Jennifer Ingrid Ray. One of Jennifer's friends, a classmate of David's, told her that she might be interested in the only law student he knew who was also a Christian. They in turn became the parents of Elsa Marie, our only grandchild, a precious gift from a gracious God!

It was about this time while the boys were still at home that we met Scamp on the Niagara Peninsula while returning from a family trip. She was part of a litter in the care of the Cushnie family. We imagined that she had the characteristics of a Gordon setter. The boys showed great interest in the pups, and the outcome was that Scamp joined our family for the remainder of the trip home. That trip and our initial acquaintance with our new member were less than auspicious. We had neglected to see to her toilet needs, and she "pooped on the floor," as the announcement came.

Scamp rapidly redeemed herself, and as she matured so did her sense of responsibility for her new family mature. She became the guardian of the property in general and more particularly the guardian of the boys. One incident will illustrate her care. Across the street from our home and one house down lived a large hound which seemed cross with the world in general and of course with other dogs in particular. The school bus stopped close by, and on one occasion Dave left our door, took a short-cut across the lawn, leaving a sad dog behind him. Both would have been happier had Dave stayed home to play! As Scamp watched her buddy cross the road, the hound took umbrage at Dave and with fierce barking bounded out toward him. That threatening action triggered some maternal instinct in little Scamp, and without a moment's hesitation she went into action, racing toward a showdown with this hound that dared to threaten her charge. The hound retreated, Dave got safely on the bus and Scamp returned in triumph to her domain, no harm done.

    She came to an untimely end, her earthly work incomplete. She used to walk with us when we ventured into the woods or down to the river nearby. On the return trip she would walk carefully between Joan and me, seeming to find security in the place of protection. At other times she would accompany me on a walk to the post office, not turning aside except for the occasional exploration of interesting smells along the side of the path, hoping to find some tasty morsel. We suspected that it was one of these samplings along the way that became cause of her distress following one of these outings. She became quite ill and in her distress crawled out into the empty field behind our home, there to face her dilemma alone. When Dave returned from school and was told about Scamp, he went out and found her, brought her in and prepared a soft bed for her on the basement floor. She died there, and was buried among some birch trees on a hill near the community cemetery.

    Wendell was something else! Named after Wendell Clark, he was contemporary with Jake and lived with Dave. His all-too-brief life was packed with adventure, the best of it, I suspect, in his fertile canine imagination. If he became bored, he might toss a ball or some other object into the air and then catch it. One of his more hilarious capers involved getting hold of Jake's leash and leading him around the yard, Jake all the while submitting meekly to such humiliation! Out on the bush trail Wendell delighted to pull out all the stops sprinting down a straight stretch of pathway, his powerful hind legs propelling him at incredible speeds and his massive shoulders bashing anything that happened to be in the way including Jake if he failed to dodge quickly enough. At the end of his dash he would pause, turn and repeat the sprint with equal vigor in the opposite direction.

    Wendell collaborated with Jake in providing training for Granny Tulloch. Granny's frequent visits were occasions of opportunity for

"I Never Did Learn to Dance"

the two dogs. They took full advantage of her leaving to appear at her car door, both on best behaviour, both looking eagerly and intently toward the source of their expected treat. Granny didn't fail them. Oatmeal cookies had been stored in preparation for the moment and were now brought out and placed in the salivating mouths of the two suppliants. They trained well and they had the advantage of an apt student.

The end for Wendell came peacefully, evidently in his sleep. Dave found him one morning lying without breath or life where he had gone to sleep the night before. He is buried beside a lake in Quebec, a short distance north of Ottawa, sadly mourned but certainly not forgotten.

Jake was John's golden retriever, a pure bred pup registered as "Hop-Around-Jake of Massawippie." He accompanied John to Germany where they lived for some seven years, both of them learning to communicate in German. On their return to Canada, Jake became a permanent resident in the senior Spears' home, a stay lasting over seven pleasant years.

Jake's stay was pleasant especially because of his compliant nature. He was easy to train. On occasion another side of his character surfaced, a side seemingly uncharacteristic for him. When allowed to range freely, he often demonstrated a condition we called selective hearing, a syndrome my father also seemed to manifest from time to time. His normally keen hearing seemed to have utterly vanished. At such times the best response was to let him go; generally he would end up at the garbage bins behind the local market, looking for stray tit-bits.

One of these excursions almost did him in and me as well. The two of us used to go for extended walks along the trail in the woods by the river near our home. Depending on the season, the river could be relatively shallow—though not shallow enough to wade without risk—or alternatively fast and deep. In winter it was often frozen over, but sometimes frozen along the edges only leaving a swift channel in the middle. It was in this latter state that we got into a challenging situation. Jake had gone on ahead and disappeared from sight; my calls brought no response. Then the reason for the silence soon became clear: a brief opening in the trees beside the river revealed the ice on both edges with the current coursing down the middle, and there at the edge of the ice was a golden head and two paws clinging desperately to the ice. My only thought then was to rescue him; later sober second thought presented alternatives, most of them with the dog carried down the river to almost certain death. I ventured onto the ice, got hold of his collar and hauled on him. The ice held, Jake clamored up and by God's mercy both of us were spared. He shook off the icy water and trotted happily down the trail. I followed, pondering just what it was that possessed me to attempt such a reckless rescue.

Jake loved games. One of his more interesting games might have been called 'Spot the Stick.' When we were on a trail in the woods and Jake often carried a short stick of wood. He would go on ahead out of sight, drop the stick on the trail and then hide in the woods nearby. His 'hiding' was hilarious! He would lie flat on the ground behind a tree, pretending to be out of sight. We never let on that we could see him. If we were sharp enough to notice the stick when we caught up, that was a point for us. If, on the other hand, we were not sufficiently observant and missed the stick, that was a point for him and he would promptly come out of hiding, retrieve it and go on ahead to set up the bait for the next test.

He also loved the snow. Occasionally he came upon a deep bank in the woods and be possessed of a notion that he wanted to investigate any life that might lurk in the depths. Snow would fly and the head would be thrust down into the hole, the hole getting deeper and the head thrust further until at last he was buried to his shoulders, great snorts coming to the surface from time to time. Any field mice would be quite safe.

A variant of this winter activity took place with the shoveling of the drive. As the piles at the edge of the drive grew higher, Jake would clamor up on top and with great effort pull back the snow to make room for more. He seemed to sense that this work was his responsibility, and indeed it was a help. Any slacking off on the part of the one shoveling and a sharp bark would get things moving again.

Jake's reputation in the community—and by association, ours—remained at a high level generally. He behaved himself well around people. One exception to this good behaviour lay in his attitude to small creatures, whether small children or small dogs. He exhibited a peculiar disregard for little animals or little children. He wasn't in the least hostile in this behaviour; just indifferent. On one occasion this disregard became an embarrassment to the family. Jake and I were on the way to the river for our usual outing in so doing passed close to a children's playground. There we encountered a grandmother with two little girls and a little dog. Jake hustled over to meet the grandmother, as always friendly with folks. Then it happened. The announcement came from one of the little girls: "He peed on our dog!" Jake had quickly lifted his leg and anointed the little guy, fulfilling whatever canine instinct that motivates such behaviour.

I had some routines in my daily habits and Jake easily adapted to them for his own benefit. Mornings were usually spent at my desk. Around eleven o'clock I could expect an interruption. If listening carefully, I might hear a soft pad on the steps or the near-silent opening of the door (conveniently left unlatched), but more often the weight of a soft nuzzle on my leg. When our eyes met the tail would wag! I seldom needed further encouragement, and my first move would signal the beginning of a delightful daily routine. At that move Jake would turn and quickly exit the den, mount the few steps to the landing, pause, turn and glance back to make sure I was fulfilling my part in the routine. The next lap took us to the entry where he waited, nose to the door while I caught up. He patiently endured the humility of having a leash attached, and then we were off.

Jake's world was serenely benign. He evidently lacked any shred of meanness or aggression, preferring to regard his environment—other dogs and people included—as if all were one big, contented family. His pacifism did have limits: any dog daring to take his stick would have to deal with a very possessive owner. Apart from this his trust was profound.

That trust remained with him to the last day of his life. That day dawned clear and bright, and it was with something of a heavy heart on my part that Jake and I went out for our usual hike in the woods behind the shopping mall. It would be our last hike together: we had an appointment with the vet for just after lunch.

The vet and I had talked about this earlier when Jake had shown some signs of failure in different parts of his system. We didn't want to see him slowly become disabled or diseased and so suffer a painful old age, and so we had spoken to him about our concern. He assured us that we could have him euthanized—and that for any reason. Jake was now beyond the average age for his breed; several little ailments were noticeable in his behaviour, and we were about to move to a high rise in the city. It seemed that the time had come. From one point of view, no time is right for death, even that of an animal, especially one that has been a welcome addition to the household for some years, but, on the other hand, death intrudes uninvited, even into human relationships that are deeper and considerably more complex than those involving animals.

So, after that final walk in the woods we set out, just the two of us, one heavy hearted, the other as trusting as ever, out for a ride to some new adventure with his master.

On this visit, unlike the many other visits to the vet, I had to deal first of all with paying the expences. They've been through this thing before. That duty attended to, we were led to one of the examining rooms where we waited. Soon a technician appeared to take Jake out for some preparatory work. They came back shortly with a device strapped with bandages to Jake's lower leg. Jake was his usual trusting self, glad to see me! Shortly afterward the doctor came with an assistant. He asked whether or not I would like to spend some final moments with Jake, and I assured him that we had our final time together that morning in the woods. He was uncharacteristically solemn. It was at this time that the Scripture passage came into mind and I asked the two of them if they remembered the words, *"He was led as a Lamb to the slaughter and as a sheep before her shearers is dumb so he does not open his mouth."* They seemed taken aback, and I explained that this was spoken of the Lord.

The veterinarian kindly explained what was about to happen, that Jake who was standing with my arm around him, still trusting, would slowly sink down to the floor as the chemicals were administered by means of the device already in place on his leg. Reminding me that this procedure was irrevocable, the doctor then proceeded to do his solemn work. It happened just as he said. Checking carefully with his stethoscope a few moments later, he said quietly, "He's gone."

'He's gone,' but he's far from forgotten. We think and speak of him often. 'He's only a dog': true, but a dog that had become a significant presence in our family routine: at the breakfast table for a treat from his mistress, or down to the study to announce to his master that it's time to go for our daily walk. He leaves an imprint, generally a very memorable and positive one. There'll not be another like him!

I had spent nearly four years working underground at Levack mine, most of that time spent drilling and blasting new tunnels or drifts, as they were called, tasks that taxed both body and soul. An escape loomed when an acquaintance suggested that I consider becoming a representative for a major life insurance company. I could trade my Standfield's woolen 'long-johns' etc. for a suit and tie! I switched, and for about three years became a sales person. Only later did I discover that I was basically unsuited for this occupation, a psychological interest test clearly indicating that persuasiveness was not my forte—indeed it was much below average. I had made a move to escape Scylla on the one hand and had fallen into Charybdis on the other. Now what? This was becoming a very unattractive pattern.

One hilarious event happened at this time. Hats suitable for me were a challenge both to me and to Joan. I had a growing collection of hats and caps of various sizes and shapes and textures but none of these got general approval. Finding the ideal head covering that pleased both of us became an ongoing challenge. Then finally the goal seemed within sight.

Keep in mind that I was now garbed in business suit and all the accessories. Well, almost all. I didn't have a suitable hat. I couldn't call on clients hatless. Fortunately a men's fine clothing shop was situated near my office. Reg. Wilkinson's carried only the best in men's clothing. There one day I found myself in the shop attended by Reg himself. He showed me the various range of hats available. One hat, however, stood out and was accompanied by his highest recommendation. Nothing would do but that I should have that hat.

The purchase made, out of the shop I marched with my newest head-covering: a beautiful brown *bowler*! In case the name is unfamiliar (It's that out-of-date!), it can be described as a round-crowned hard felt hat, named after its designer. Its top was shaped like a bowl fitted with a narrow brim. It was evidently in fashion in 1850 when it first appeared but hardly in vogue a century and more later! There is a kind of rich humour involved in the exchange of the necessary hard hat in the mine for the century-old bowler in the office. My colleagues there were merciful. Suffice it to say that I never wore out the new hat. It was pawned off to the first interested acquaintance.

It is somewhat remarkable that the search for hats still persists, half a century later. I'm a little more buyer-resistant now.

That same psychological test revealed innate abilities that would enable me to undertake a range of endeavors, university education being one surprising option. Clearly anything involving the need for persuasiveness was not recommended. As a consequence, I soon found myself enrolled in the first year of courses at Laurentian University. My acceptance was conditional: as an adult student, permission to continue subsequent years' study was contingent upon my having passed four out of the first six courses undertaken. I was able to continue, very conscious of my role as an interloper. Worse was yet to come.

I had not yet completed my university work when a series of circumstances (Coincidences again?) resulted in an offer of employment teaching English in a local high school. The outcome was that I found myself one of a Secondary School teaching staff, ready to take up assigned duties in an English classroom. Inevitably the moment came when I faced my first class—Grade 10 General Level. Not only was it my first class that morning; it was my first time in a normal Secondary School English class! Grade eight in Tobermory was my final year in formal classes, though three years of Bible school and a few night school courses in Hamilton helped to round out my scanty academic qualifications. The skilled interloper survived that first year as a teacher of English and nineteen subsequent years.

I have lived much of my life carrying with me a vague and largely unexamined sense that I am an interloper. This awareness lurks far below the daily consciousness and only surfaces occasionally. But it's there. The term interloper is defined as an intruder, "one who (especially for profit) thrusts himself into others' affairs; (Hist.) unauthorized trader" (Concise Oxford Dictionary).

What's the evidence for the reality of the presence of this unattractive aspect of character?

Probably the earliest remembrance is that of being alone while in the midst of a family. My older siblings were quite out of my age range and my experience, the nearest being my sister, twelve years my senior. My younger brother was born with Down's syndrome and we had little meaningful companionship. My parents were both busy with the affairs of life—my father running a lumbering business and my mother seeing to the maintenance of the farm home and the family. Consequently I didn't have the sense that I was a welcomed member of the family unit. I came along and they did what they needed to do to accommodate the new arrival.

I didn't thrust myself into this situation, but felt thrust into it nevertheless. I had intruded myself (by whatever governing circumstances then active—"There's a Divinity that shapes our ends/rough-hew them how we will") into the life of this busy family and now must necessarily make the most of it. This is not at all to suggest that I was not provided for or that I was abused in any way. Indeed quite the contrary is the case. It is simply the impression gained when trying to rightly see the dominant features of that experience many decades ago.

Living on a farm entails its own sense of isolation, both good and otherwise. Sport became a welcome companion in those days. This black and white collie nearly got himself killed facing a young bear while protecting me. He recovered from his wounds and lived for years after. The bear suffered a different fate at the hands of two uncles armed with axes, and his tanned hide provided a rug for my bedroom.

The family move from the farm to the village when I was about six years of age didn't do much to allay my sense of alienation. The village had its own society, and though I did have friends my own age, I never felt thoroughly at home there.

The Hamilton scene provides a good example of the interloper at work. There I found myself in the proximity of the saintly Cushnie family. Because I had become friends with George Cushnie who was my age, they took me in almost as though I were one with them. I certainly didn't thrust myself on this family, but I did take advantage of the opportunity to be part this loving group. This association persisted for years and I recognize in retrospect that this was (apart from my mother) my first encounter with genuine Christians.

"I Never Did Learn to Dance"

There too in the city of Hamilton I encountered the folks at the Delta Tabernacle where I made a false profession of being a Christian believer in order to avoid an unpleasant situation and to fit into the fellowship there without too many questions being asked. This scenario came about in the following manner.

My adoptive family, the Cushnies, took me along with them to Sunday church services at the Delta Tabernacle in Hamilton. Here it was that I heard from the pulpit teachings that were strange to me. I had always been taught that in this matter of pleasing God one must do the best one can; God is decent and he understands that we're not perfect. But now at the Delta I was confronted by the teaching that apart from the grace of God we are all lost sinners in his sight. Furthermore, the only way to access a right standing before God was to be born again! I just didn't get it. Yet even though I wasn't convinced intellectually by what I heard, I could not dismiss the whole thing. The godly lives of the people involved—the Cushnies and the folks at the Delta—proved to be a more powerful influence in the long run. Above all these evident circumstances and the shaping of my eternal destiny was the grace and loving purpose of God.

The crisis came on the occasion of some special evangelistic meetings at the church. A certain Dr. Hunter was the speaker. As usual I attended along with the family, and on this Sunday evening I found myself sitting beside Mr. Cushnie. The meeting came to its conclusion with the traditional altar call, and I was ready for the final "Amen" and a quick exit. It was not to be, and the details of this episode in the journey of the interloper are recorded elsewhere.

Another clear example of the interloper at work occurred not too long after marriage. It was then that I, a school drop-out at the end of grade eight, found myself attending classes in Laurentian University. An even more glaring example followed when I for the first time in my life set foot in a regular grade nine English classroom—as the teacher! (I had in the meantime earned three secondary school credits through night school courses.) Some twenty years later I retired from teaching, now free to reveal my dark secret to my colleagues. I said nothing. I suspect that interlopers generally don't brag about their intrusions. V. S. Naipaul in Half a Life has one of his characters reflecting on his choices in life: "It sometimes happens when you make a slip of the tongue you don't want to correct it. You try to pretend that what you said was what you meant."

Is it possible to be an interloper after fifty years taking part in a church congregation? Whether or not I was an interloper at Larchwood Bible Chapel in the judgment of others may be debatable, but that subconscious awareness was not far below the surface. It was surely in part because of the patriarchal substructure of the church that I found myself in a virtually compromising situation. It was not that the milieu was chafing and certainly not that it was doctrinally compromising. It was just that I didn't wholeheartedly fit in. The obvious question is, why did I stay? The answer may not satisfy others, but for me it was a case that I felt that the Lord had placed me there and I was unwilling to move, though the possibility cropped up more than once and one time seriously. A teaching position in Meaford seemed attractive, with the blue waters of Georgian Bay beckoning.

Ultimately the nudge to move became stronger and the motivating factors more complex and compelling. The irony is that I am more than ever an interloper here in Ottawa! Maybe that's life. Maybe it's like the colour of one's skin: it's with you wherever you go. Persevere!

It was while we were living in Ottawa that the following episode occurred in which the interloper had a narrow escape, an episode either alarming or hilarious, depending on where you sit--literally.

An unexpected phone call from our son and daughter-in-law inviting us to go along with them and Elsa for a quick trip to Montreal, especially to visit the Biodome, a destination just a little short of heaven for Elsa who seems intrigued by anything living.

"I Never Did Learn to Dance"

We arrived at the Biodome early so as to miss the crowds. While others were purchasing tickets, I decided to visit the men's room to make myself comfortable in view of the exploration of what promised to be a very impressive display. A helpful young man behind a counter gave me directions: "You will find what you're looking for on the next level down. The elevator is just over there." He notices that the stairs might be a challenge for me. The elevator itself was a challenge, as it had letters and symbols attached to buttons giving directions.

All was quiet on the basement level. Not a soul was in sight. Looking around for my destination, I spotted this wide open doorway and inside some sinks and cubicles. Surely this is it; maybe they do things differently here. I go in and pass an unusual number of cubicles before arriving at the one I want: the one designed for handicapped folks. I enter and fortunately lock the door. All remained quiet on this unoccupied floor.

Then came the unexpected: the sound of distant voices, feminine voices, voices of mothers and their daughters. The voices grew closer and the realization came withe chilling realization that people were coming into this toilet area and that these people were female. The truth dawned : I had inadvertently wandered into the ladies' toilet.

More and more voices filled the area. The place was getting quite busy. One visitor attempted to get into my cubicle. Panic threatened. I'm trapped. What if she speaks? I search my mind for any possible means of escape. How long can I stay like this? How can I get out of here with any shred of dignity left? If I make a dash for it, what kind of reaction will this provoke among the ladies and children? Will they call security? Yet I can't wait indefinitely here, trapped in this cubicle.

The came the possible way of escape. The voices retreated and for the moment all became silent. Was this an answer to prayer? I reckoned so and hoped for the best. I opened the door of my prison cell, glanced furtively around and made a hasty withdrawal:

past the seemingly endless row of cubicles (Why hadn't the reality dawned on me earlier?) past the washbasins and out the still opened doorway. No one was around.

A quick retreat to the safety of the mens' room farther down the hallway provided opportunity for a clean-up and for catching my breath. I breathed a thanksgiving and rejoined the others. The interloper had narrowly escaped the consequences of his unintended intrusion.

And then there is that oft-recurring, oppressive dream in which I find myself back in the educational setting. The very frequency and persistence of the phenomenon must be significant. In my dream, I inevitably I find myself ill-prepared for my task and therefore facing a make-do situation. Not only so, but my authorities, though at times unseen, are not far away, and are ready to find and expose my incompetence. Freud would no doubt have an easy time with this scenario. I would be interested in his diagnosis.

It might well be argued that as a Gentile I am an interloper on a truly grand scale within that unnumbered company of God's saints. The apostle Paul argues in Romans 11 that Gentiles have been *"grafted in"* to the cultivated olive tree that is Israel. They don't naturally belong there in that privileged position. Some of the natural branches have been broken off and we Gentiles have slipped in to take their place—indeed to occupy a more wonderful place. We are interlopers to a magnificent degree!

David suggests this in Psalm 39:

"For I dwell with You as an alien,
A stranger as all my fathers were." (v. 12b)

Even David, the man after God's own heart and part of the chosen people, seemed conscious of the distance between himself and the God of creation. He says again:

Who am I, O Sovereign Lord, and what is my family,
that you have brought me this far?
And as if this were not enough in your sight, O Sovereign Lord,

you have also spoken about the future of the house of your servant. Is this your usual way of dealing with man, O Sovereign Lord?" 2 Samuel 7:18f.

Little wonder that David was a worshipper!

Other Old Testament characters echo a similar theme: Ruth the Moabitess was something of an interloper. She recognized and confessed that she was a "foreigner" in Israel. When she was graciously welcomed by the wealthy Boaz, she exclaimed to her benefactor, *"Why have I found such favour in your eyes that you notice me—a foreigner?"* Moses felt like he had *"become an alien in a foreign land,"* and marked this awareness in the family records by naming his son Gershom, a name sounds like the Hebrew for "an alien there." (Exodus 18:3)

The Lord Jesus, speaking prophetically in Psalm 69:8, says: *"I am a stranger to my brothers, an alien to my own mother's sons."* Our Lord wasn't an interloper here in this world, but he certainly knew what it was to be rejected. *"He was in the world, and though the world was made through him, the world did not recognize him. He came to that which was his own, but his own did not receive him."* One of the more poignant moments in the Lord's sojourn here occurred when many of his disciples turned back and no longer followed him. It was then that he said to the Twelve who remained with him, *"You do not want to leave too, do you?"* At the end of that journey lay the cross, the ultimate rejection, an exclusion of cosmic consequences.

Then I read in Colossians chapter one that *"the . . . Father has qualified you ['made you fit,' JND] to share in the inheritance of the saints in the kingdom of light. For He has rescued us from the dominion of darkness and brought us into the kingdom of the Son He loves, in whom we have redemption, the forgiveness of sins."* Here I can legitimately substitute the first person 'me' for the second person 'you': the Father has made me, the interloper, fit!

God the Father has already dealt with the darkness and the distance and the alienation, all of which were my portion. This

He did through the cross where our Lord knew fully what it was to be thrust into an immeasurable distance for those brief, dark hours. Not only so, not only has the Father rescued us, but He has brought us in, in from the alienation and from the distance, in to share in some wonderful way the kingdom that is rightly only the Son's. Somehow this interloper has lost his sense of alienation and found a welcome, a legitimate welcome in the kingdom of light, and that by virtue of Christ's work on the cross. It's truly an occasion for heartfelt thanksgiving!

Retirement followed twenty years of teaching, an early retirement made possible by the Board's need to move older, more expensive teachers from service. Twenty years of helping in the local assembly in various ways involving spiritual exercises followed.

Opportunities to travel also followed retirement. An invitation to join three other men on a trip to Columbia provided an opportunity to see the so-called Third World first hand. Kurt Ruby, a former missionary to Columbia, was returning to revisit friends and colleagues there. I was eager to go.

The first leg of the journey took our neighbour Ron Ramsay and me to Toronto where we waited our plane to Miami. Ron's journey came perilously close to being aborted there, as he suffered a severe reaction to medication for tropical ailments and ended up in hospital. On we went to Miami where we enjoyed our final salads of the trip. We were warned to scrupulously avoid raw fruits and vegetables while in Columbia. The temptation to indulge came often and came powerfully, but caution prevailed. I escaped with only one easily manageable midnight bout of intestinal distress.

From one limited point of view, Columbia was a land of contrasts. On the one hand, elaborate homes garrisoned about by high steel fences or masonry walls topped by imbedded glass shards lined some boulevards in the cities. On the other hand, peasants were often seen on the streets, trying to sell odds and ends in order to eke out a living. I only saw the surface of Columbian society;

"I Never Did Learn to Dance"

what lay hidden underneath? Is there a relationship between a nation that has embraced Christianity and its consequent material prosperity and one that has generally remained in spiritual darkness and suffers social injustice? The WASP factor may have a sound historical basis.

This world system cries out for fundamental social justice, but that cry will not be fully answered until reign of Christ, God's anointed King. *"I have installed my King on Zion, my holy hill,"* we read in Psalm 2. This prophetic Scripture speaks of God's Son, once crucified here by the very ones He came to save. In God's sovereign purposes and foreknowledge, His Christ is already enthroned. Though the time of that public presentation remains in the Father's discretion, its appearance with all its attendant majestic glory is utterly certain.

Travel in Columbia revealed one rather ominous side of life in that society. An incident on an overnight bus trip provides illustration. Kurt had quietly indicated the extended nails on the hand of a man sitting near us. "Groomed for picking pockets," Kurt said. It was later in the capital city of Bogota that the four of us were crossing an intersection when I had a first-hand encounter with these highly skilled operatives.

The lead three men in our group had already reached the curb and I had just stepped up from the street onto the sidewalk. The opening movement in the little drama that followed consisted of a rather firm collision with a man approaching from my right side. Earnest protests of apology followed as this man engaged me, evidently to seek my pardon for his carelessness. While I was attempting to reassure this man with his animated gestures, an accomplice was at my left side attempting to extract my passport from my side pants' pocket. Fortunately for me, the passport caught slightly on its way from its place, and I looked to see the cause. A rather slight Columbian man with a guilty look stood there. My immediate response was most revealing: here was I, a Christian in a foreign country, seeking to be a witness to "the pagans" there and an encouragement to other believers; and my reaction to this incident? I wanted to seize this offender's arm with two hands and break it over my knee! I had already passed judgment on this man at my side. God, however, allowed me to glimpse what was in my heart. By nature we weren't that different, this Columbian and I; he attempting to steal my property, and I angry enough to think of breaking his arm! Who carried the greater guilt?

That same journey yielded a few other memorable moments. The missionaries we had visited and the ones we were to meet were not 'employed' by any organization; that is, they didn't get a regular paycheck. They did, of course, receive funds from individuals and churches, often through such entities as Missionary Service Committee. They would profess to live by the principle that God supplies his laborers with sufficient funds for their needs. Kurt and I engaged in a discussion as we traveled as to principles underlying living by faith—i.e., trusting God alone to supply the needs—versus the need to establish a base—i.e., develop a constituency through which one would be supported. I was quite adamant that trust in God was sufficient. He would meet his servant's needs. A similar case arose in Nigeria with Fred regarding funds for well-drilling equipment. I was persuaded that it would honour God simply to ask him only to supply the need. I might be less adamant now. Both these men had experience trusting the Lord, Fred for half a century, including the establishment, development and ongoing service of Parkside Ranch.

Our bus inexplicably stopped along a deserted section of the highway in the middle of the night. This brought me to full wakefulness. Kurt had told us stories of armed thugs stopping vehicles, of gold teeth being yanked out of mouths—were they just stories? Armed men entered the bus and were coming down the aisle toward us. I tried to make myself look inconspicuous. My concern, however, in this case was unnecessary. These men were looking for drug runners. They soon left.

How memorable could a cup of coffee possibly be? This one in Columbia was unique. We had traveled through the night on this bus and were tired and cold. Just as the first streaks of daylight were illuminating the surrounding mountain peaks, we neared our destination. The city lay below, and our driver pulled off to the parking lot of a coffee shop. There I was introduced to a mug of steaming hot café aux lait. Strong, hot and sweet! Never before and never since have I so enjoyed this Columbian beverage. No doubt the circumstances enhanced the experience.

Reflections from a six-week stay at Ika, Nigeria, April and May 1991

It's 8 o'clock in the evening of our first full day at the mission station at Ika, Benue State, Nigeria. It's already dark—the sun equitably marking the twelve hours of day and night. The trip that began at 24 Leonard Street at 7:20 a.m. Tuesday, April 23, Peter's Birthday, ended here last evening, April 25, at 9:30.

The British Airways desks at Pearson's #3 Terminal were surrounded by large displays advertising BA's "Up and Away Day." Entertainers of various sorts with music and costumes appeared and drew a small and curious crowd, including Fred Warnholtz and myself. On inquiry we learned that all passengers flying BA anywhere in the world on April 23 were traveling courtesy the Airline and that included us, we learned, even though we had already paid our fare!

Our luggage was a different matter—not our personal luggage, but the 1/4 ton supply of material we had agreed to carry to Nigeria, including two engines for lawn mowers! The engines were in the light cartons; boxes of books for the school on the mission station caused some consternation and negotiation. We finally were required to pay for only two extra bags.

Our flights were uneventful, and included in the final leg from London an interesting session with a Nigerian Air Lines pilot from the Housa tribe, dressed in typical full length loose white shirt over trousers. He was a Muslim living in Bauchi State, very friendly, giving his name, address and phone number, should I get to his city. It was only the next day that we learned that the BBC had broadcast news of Muslim-'Christian' riots in Bauchi, with perhaps as many as 80 people being killed and many churches burned. Our informants, staff at a Christian College in Jos, added that "they" were only some 17 km away. Some refugee survivors had arrived destitute at the College a few hours before, and were being given food and shelter. This kind of information added a bit of adrenalin to the bloodstream, and gave an added appreciation of the lot of God's servants on the front lines and of our own security at home.

Our arrival in Kano after a flight from London underscored two aspects of the land of Nigeria: its proximity to the desert, creeping down from the north, and its "always hot" climate. (It was 41 c. when we stepped off the plane, with a wind from the desert intensifying the heat.) Our departure from Kano six weeks later was marked by an event that also characterized the climatic nature of northern Nigeria—the coming of the 'Harmattan,' a wind from the north-east carrying with it the dust and sand of the Sahara. It was late on a hot and dry Sunday afternoon, and we had just arrived in Kano. The sky took on a peculiar murky-yellowish hue and the wind began to blow. What followed in the hour or so that it lasted was what we would have described as a dust storm, and that in the city. Anyone caught outside in this situation would have to cover his face to breathe. Rain arrived to rinse the dust from the air, and it ended as abruptly as it had begun.

Fine, multi-story, modern buildings co-exist with rather primitive market areas in the larger cities. Within an hour's drive of Kano, mud-brick thatched roof dwellings indicate the homes of people belonging to one of Nigeria's 250 or more tribes. Overhead fly the 747's of Nigerian Airways, while out in the fields men, women and children stoop in hard labour with the grub-hoe in order to eke out a scant existence from the land.

"I Never Did Learn to Dance"

Tom Wheeler had arranged for an agent to see us through customs, an immensely helpful measure, especially in our circumstances with our 500 pounds of baggage. Tom and his wife Lois (Dibble) have been serving the Lord at Ika since 1978, and live on the Mission Station with their five children. Lois's parents, Spencer and Phyllis Dibble have been laboring there since 1954. Tom managed to pack all our stuff into the Peugeot 425 station wagon (newly reconditioned by him), and we set off through a market section of Kano before settling into our rooms for the night. This was our introduction to Nigeria—and to the "Weaver-bird" in the courtyard of our motel, a bird that weaves a hanging nest with the opening at the bottom and to one side—a marvel of ornithological engineering, I thought.

The trip south was long and wearying, some sections of the highway laced with pot-holes and demanding the utmost skill in navigation by our very capable driver. Mud-walled homes with thatched roofs nestled behind the walls of little communities along the route. Savannah land—bare, dry soil dotted with a few trees here and there—lay waiting the coming rainy season when a crop of corn would flourish. Savannah gave way to forests and hills, some quite high, as we rose to the plateau section of central Nigeria, with Jos as its capital.

Frequent police checks slowed our journey, one of which promised trouble. On being questioned, we were ordered to show what we carried. Our hearts were heavy as contemplated the ¼ ton of North American goods being unloaded and displayed there on the highway. We got out prepared for the worst. A sudden sharp command from a policeman at the car behind ours caught everyone's attention: "Bring guns!" We were hastily waved on while the police extricated three young men at gun point. We thanked God for His timely intervention, took fresh courage and drove away.

Tiny pinpoints of flickering light in Igala darkness along the road disclosed the fires of families relaxing around the evening meal as we approached the mission area. The final few jolting kilometers into Ika introduced us to bush roads in Nigeria, and this was one of the better ones.

God's work in Benue (now Koji) State, began over 70 years ago with the arrival of Mr. and Mrs. Raymond Dibble, missionaries from America. Pioneer missionary and Bible translator, Mr. Dibble first brought the good news of Christ to the tribes of this area. An old man, recognized as the first convert to Christ in this part of Nigeria, attended a service of thanksgiving at Ika while we were there. Still vigorous in old age, he spoke movingly to the large gathering at the mission station. Translations of the Scripture by Mr. Dibble into the local languages, a monumental task for any one man, continue in use to this day. The earthly remains of God's pioneer servant lie buried close to the scene of the conference, waiting the "last trumpet" call.

Cock-crow in the pre-dawn darkness came at about five a.m. (Was it the same in Israel 2000 years ago, I wondered?) These soloists were soon joined by a chorus of lyrical forest voices greeting the arrival of the new day. Later, in May, the strong male voices of the Bible school students would raise their cheery matins to the Lord at about six o'clock: "I have decided to follow Jesus," sounded through the mission grounds, though the words are in Igala. They love to sing.

Our introduction to missionary work involved some rags and brushes for cleaning, a paint brush and a pail of paint, a medical clinic unused for years, now badly in need of refurbishing inside and out, made fit for the Master's use and for the benefit of the local inhabitants. The keys to the clinic had been returned to the missionaries just at the time of our arrival, and great interest attended the prospective opening of medical facilities that had been dormant for years. Forty or so of the sick and injured began to gather under the sun-shelter in front of the clinic on the first day, scarcely before restoration work had begun. Good news travels fast.

"I Never Did Learn to Dance"

Besides the medical work which includes a very busy maternity wing, the mission station at Ika is involved in ongoing translation and revision activities, publishing of Bible School materials, hymn books, correspondence courses and other publications as well as the Bible School itself, a major undertaking in which 70 or 80 men and women come to Ika for a month of intensive study of God's Word. Capable native teachers assist Spenser in this work during a number of these months throughout the year. Up-to-date computer equipment would greatly ease the load, cut down the time involved, and increase the quality of the product in many of these areas.

Life is fragile and precarious here. A baby dies on the way home because the medication given the mother for the baby is not administered soon enough. A young woman suffers from an infected heal, pierced by a thorn; a man has blood poison in his hand. On another late afternoon a some days later, we were painting at the clinic and had just about finished for the day. A small knot of ladies from the nearby village remained under the corrugated-iron covered shelter. Oosamon, the medical technician from a neighboring centre, disappeared into the middle of the group, remained for a time, and then reappeared and left the clinic. Moments later a loud, piercing wail arose from the midst the group. One of the ladies seemed to be in acute pain and threw herself to the ground, the others struggling to help her. They assisted her to walk, still wailing, toward the adjacent village, her grieving cries receding into the evening. Her little baby had just died. Life is fragile indeed.

A door of opportunity for trained medical personnel lies open at Ika. The facilities are there, the need is there, fine accommodations are in place, and an abundant supply of well water is expected early in the new-year, thanks in part to the exercises of Fred Warnholtz, who saw the need and made it known to God's people here in the homeland.

It's Friday, and we don clean shirts in honor of our audience before the head man of Ika. He is expecting us, and it is a mark of courtesy to attend; we are in his territory, and we must not disregard the invitation.

We travel by car to Ika, though it is really contiguous with the mission compound. The main 'street'—a mere wide path amid mud-walled homes—is home to a variety of colours and sizes of goats which scamper out of our way. We stop before a larger structure—perhaps 25-30 feet across the front—that is headquarters and home to the Chief of the Ika area, an area comprising about 20,000 souls. Two doors stand open, revealing a darkened interior; the door to the right is ours. On entering we note a figure seated on the far side of the room in a large chair befitting his bulk and office. He doesn't rise to greet us, but he does welcome us in good English for a Nigerian in this area. We go through the customary Igala: How are you? How are your wives? How are your children? The Chief assures us that we are most welcome in his area. The fact that medical facilities are to become available to benefit his people is not lost on him.

He wears trousers beneath a lengthy, loose winding of brightly colored material, one shoulder remaining bare. His feet are sandaled. His eyes are bloodshot, and he is somewhat obese, quite unusual for a Nigerian. When we ask how many children he has, he laughs easily! He's not sure; probably around seventeen, from his seven wives who occupy the apartments that enclose the courtyards behind. Five boys ranging in age from five to eight sit on a bench at the far end of the long room we occupy. One three year old lad, quite unencumbered by any stitch of clothing, sits near his father. The Chief discourses easily, asking questions about Canada, the snow and education. He has been twice to Mecca, an important pilgrimage for a devout Muslim, and an indication of his status in the community.

It is Saturday, about 4 p.m., and the rain had begun as we set out on our first safari. Travel is on the main highway, a fine new one, most of the way, then on a narrow dirt road—two ruts—at times with pools of water wider than the tracks; we ease our way through hoping that bottom is not too far down. There are farms along the way, with houses near the road. These farms are really cultivated areas among the trees where crops are already springing up: ground nuts (peanuts), yams, and cassava, responding to the rainy season already beginning. Houses are mud brick, many with corrugated roofs. We pass a small community with a marketplace, the stalls unoccupied at the time.

Always along the roads people are walking; one or two or a small group, the women carrying the burdens on their heads. They are erect and stately in their walk, their heads held high and steady as they swing gracefully along under their loads. Colorful garments swathe them to ankle length, and bright scarves cover their hair.

Isaac has been waiting to join us and guide us through the final few kilometers of difficult terrain to our destination. We announce our arrival by horn and are met by a crowd that follows our Land Rover to a stop. A solid bank of young black faces, scarcely discernible in the gathering darkness, is discovered by the myriad pairs of eye-whites; they watch us intently. They are not rude—indeed quite otherwise, almost to the point of embarrassment—just simply curious. Not many whites visit them, and indeed their own civic officials don't trouble themselves to venture so far into the bush. Their welcome is genuine.

A generous meal is served: a large container of boiled yam, a potato-like vegetable and an important part of their diet, is accompanied by a dish of savory sauce. Custom here dictates that a portion is pulled from the large lump of yam and rolled into a ball with the right hand only, then dipped into this sauce of unknown ingredients, though hot pepper is evidently one. Breakfast is of the leftover yam, but this time sliced and fried. It is quite edible with a bit of marmalade from 'home.'

This is a "Good News" visit, and meetings are held only on Saturday evening and Sunday morning, though that Lord's Day was begun with a baptism at a convenient spring reached by a ten minute walk and a steep descent to a quiet pool outside the village. One teenage believer followed the Lord in obedience to His Word that day.

The more substantial conferences begin with a trip out to location on a Wednesday afternoon. One such occasion that we spent on trek involved a four hour ride out into the bush to visit a community of about two thousand souls. The final stretch of the journey was incredibly rough, and we were thankful for the 4WD Land Rover and its air conditioned interior. We crested some wooded hills, thankful that the heavy rains had not yet begun here turning red clay ruts into greasy slides, and viewed our destination nestled in a lush valley surrounded by verdant hills. Nigeria is quite attractive here, and just over the adjacent hills to the north the Benue River flows westward to join the Niger on its journey to the sea. Between the river and our hills lies a fertile plain. Well watered and prosperous, it supplies the district with food.

We arrive to the usual welcome and unload our gear—or rather have it unloaded by willing and eager hands—and set up our quarters for the next four nights. We will stay in the meeting house used by the believers in the area, now cleared and cleaned for our visit. It's a simple rectangular structure, about 20x40 feet, with cement floor, plastered mud-brick walls and corrugated iron roof. Although it appears quite vacant, the darkness reveals other interesting inhabitants: numerous bats and a few geckoes all doing a much appreciated work keeping the insect population under control. We sleep on cots, each under a suspended mosquito net that is carefully tucked in for safety. The nights provide some relief from the constant heat and humidity of Nigeria. One night also provided a sudden awakening when I was startled out a deep sleep by a loud "bang," sat up and blurted out, "What's that?" "Just a mango," Spenser replied out of the darkness. The lofty mango trees on the hillside were heavy with ripening fruit, and one of these had descended to strike the tin roof with drum-like effects inside.

"I Never Did Learn to Dance"

These falling fruits tend to be more of a nuisance when they come down and disturb the concentration of those seated in the shade during conference meetings. They are otherwise quickly retrieved and eaten by the young people, a prized and succulent snack.

Greetings are important in Nigeria: the Igala "A-wa" or the variant "AB-wa"; or the Idoma "MMM-a," are all spoken at a relatively high tonal register. The languages are tonal. "DOW-do" is used to indicate respect toward an older person. These greetings are repeated at least three times as an indication of sincerity and warmth. The senior speaker breaks off these repetitions, although they are occasionally taken up again during a lull in the conversation.

The Christians are open, friendly, and outwardly respectful in the extreme. Young men and children show great respect for their elders. The handshake is often done with his left hand holding his own right wrist. Frequently they bend the knee and head. The young women curtsey shyly as they greet an older man or even a white woman. Phyllis was sitting by the door in the evening and some of us were relaxing in the living room. Two young ladies in colorful garb approached the entry and indicated their desire to speak with Phyl. Both greeted her with the usual curtsy, words of greeting, and handshake, and then the taller of the two crouched low at Phyl's side, and with bowed head and quiet, earnest and warm smile talked for a few moments. She then rose, and both girls left with appropriate parting phrases. Phyl told us later that the taller girl was explaining why her sister hadn't greeted her at the conference. She had begged that Phyl's "heart wouldn't be spoiled" by the omission.

The elders of these believers in the bush communities are an impressive group of seniours who seem to hold positions of earned respect from all. Their faces are studies in character; I longed for a close-up film image of each. They are sober and vigilant, sitting near the speaker's table, listening closely to what is spoken, not hesitating to interrupt the speaker to correct any perceived error.

These shepherds keep watch over the flock God has entrusted to them.

The conference gatherings take place in the open air, under shade trees and under the tree-frond shelter set up for the occasion, a sun screen because of the heat and the lengthy meetings: nine to twelve each morning (three speakers); the same from three to six in the afternoon. Mid-day siesta is always welcomed! Spenser will show a gospel film for the general populous of the community in the evening while I have a 'splash bath' and rest, pleasantly weary after a busy day, wondering how this man of God endures the pace, year after year.

We speak by "interruption"; first English, then Igala, and then Idoma or Bassa or some other language. Some of the challenges facing the missionaries become apparent when it is realized that well over 400 distinct languages are spoken in this country of over 100 million souls, a population made up of about 48% Muslims, mainly in the north; about 33% 'Christian' and 18% pagan, all in the more than 250 different tribes. How to unite this diversity into a single nation remains an ongoing challenge for the Nigerian people in this oft-troubled land. Surely only the presence and kingdom of God's Christ will provide a lasting solution.

People come to these conferences bringing their seats or benches with them. Blankets are often spread on the ground to provide seating. Children and babies are also included, the infants packed very efficiently on their mother's backs, seemingly quite content. Feeding the babies is "on demand" and with little or no fuss or crying. Goats of assorted color and size also attend the meetings, moving about without notice, as do the hens with their little flocks. A practical relaxation together with a respectful order characterize the gathering; one tired of sitting will rise, stretch, and take his seat again.

It was at this conference that God revealed His loving provision in a small but encouraging way. I had neglected to bring with me any Nigerian currency, and had resigned myself to facing the prospect of sitting at the Lord's Supper with nothing to put in the bag. During a break in the meetings, a sister came up to me with the usual greetings but also with a ten nira note which she placed in my hand. This had never happened before nor did it happen after. I thanked her and the Lord for His provision—not that I had want, but it met the needs of the occasion. That occasion soon presented itself during a visit to the home of the local chief, a Muslim who graciously welcomed us and, after due compliments concerning the fine character of the Christians in his village, placed before us a present of fruits and vegetables. I remembered the ten nira note and handed it to Spenser, asking him to offer it to the chief in payment for his gift. Spen complied, and the response was immediate, predictable and firm: We were in his in his village and in his home; we were as his family and under his care. Payment was out of the question. Spen made the most of the opportunity, and the chief listened intently as the grace and Gift of God were set forth before this follower of Islam. We took our gifts—and the ten nira to be used later—and left the chief to mull over what he had heard of God's good news.

My seniour class in the May session of the Bible School at Ika met at 7:30 a.m., a good time of the day. Fifteen men and five women—ages ranging from late teens to early forties—gather to consider the Scriptures under the theme "Running to Win," from 1 Corinthians. They are serious students, mostly farmers, taking time out from their planting and cultivating year to study God's Word. They are shy and earnest, quite unsophisticated and unlettered, with an easy sense of humor lying just below the surface. There is great laughter when I use the wrong tone in referring to a student by name, and call him by the name of a fruit-bearing tree of their forest! I laugh with them when I've been instructed. They're very appreciative of any effort to help them. I was quite overwhelmed when at the conclusion of the classes they came with a collection they had taken out of the poverty of their group, a love gift that I hadn't the heart to refuse.

A visit to a local secondary school at Ika provided another side to our Nigerian venture. The vice-principal of the school had been at the chief's home on the occasion of our visit there, and he later invited me to visit the school and speak to the student assembly. I arrived a few minutes early and was escorted to the staff room. About five men were sitting at desks around the room, marking papers or attending other duties. Some animosity was evident, not surprising in this profession. I empathized with the one Christian present. One of them would like me to see that their needs in Nigeria are made known in Canada in order that we may send them help; we're very wealthy in their eyes. Another teacher demands that an orphanage be built at the mission station at Ika. I remind them that our country sends millions of dollars in aid to Africa, much of this to places like Ethiopia, far worse off than they are. They're not convinced. They surprise me later by using the assembly as a public forum for airing their deep-seated grievance. A scoffer among the staff openly ridicules the biblical teachings concerning the second coming of Christ and gains a response of laughter from the students in the audience.

Some students ask about Canada—methods of farming, discrimination, prejudice, etc.; I tell them that I was prejudiced toward Nigeria before coming there, and that such ignorance is dispelled by enlightenment. I point out how Canada has evolved from a so-called Christian country into what it is today—a mix of many cultures, religions and life-styles demanding a good deal of tolerance from all. This is front line work. I enjoy the challenge and am sorry when my time is up.

An invitation to attend a session of the district court in nearby Angpa provided an opportunity to see yet another aspect of this most interesting land. We arrived at 9 a.m. at the Court House, a long, low, corrugated-roofed building with the customary louvered windows wide open. A concrete gutter under the eaves caught and safely carried away the run-off from the down-pour that arrived with us. The din of the rain on the metal roof challenged the participants in the court proceedings, and a lawyer moved closer to the judge in order to hear and to be heard.

   We entered by a side door of the building and took our seats on one of the three benches immediately to our right. The benches have no backs. The back of the judge's chair is visible above the raised enclosure at the front of the room. Below and in front of this is a second enclosure in which are what appear to be two clerks sitting. Between these two enclosures is a bench like ours where the accused will sit, facing the judge. A uniformed official enters through a side door at the front and commands, "All rise"; the judge follows him and mounts to the Bench to take his seat. He is youthful in appearance, striking in facial features, trim of build. His eyes are alert, moving quickly to survey his court; his lips suggest a stately bearing, easily breaking into a gentle smile. No hint of weakness is evident in his remarkably open features. Incisive questions—all in English in this officially English speaking nation—to both lawyers reveal a quick mind behind a serene countenance. He seems well suited to wear the wig that covers his hair and marks his judicial office, and I imagine he must be a Christian. I'm startled when Phyl later tells me that he is pagan—very much so!

   We stayed in the Colonel's summer residence during a conference at Ogobia, a home used only a month or so a year. It was a bit down-at-heel, but luxurious by Nigerian standards, and even '4Star' compared to our usual conference accommodations. The Colonel's brother, a Christian, saw to our needs while we were there. We heard snatches of information about our absent landlord, all marked by some deference and respect.

   It was Sunday after lunch and we were all relaxing, conference duties past. Then we heard the voice, and in a moment the doorway was filled with this expansive presence: the Colonel had arrived! He was clothed in a rich, light colored two-piece garment that covered his large frame. He wasn't fat; just big. His face was round and jovial, like the image of a man at the pinnacle of his career. Geniality flowed from his eyes as he greeted each of us, Spen first (who had risen from his arm chair—a first in my company—and an indication of the weight the Colonel carried) and me last. His English was superior by Nigerian standards and he made good use of it. He had come to deliver an invitation for all of us including the Wheelers to visit his home for a dinner.

It was later that we arrived at his residence in what might be called the centre of the city (about 200,000 including the area) and were welcomed into a large living room lined with upholstered seating around the perimeter, a circular glass-topped table in the centre. We were offered refreshment of delicious, chilled, fresh mango juice after the usual preliminary and culturally obligatory greetings. We were repeatedly assured of a welcome. Our host disappeared into a back room and reappeared moments later with a rough, round, black object in his hand. He then announced with appropriate ceremony that what he is about to do is a traditional Nigerian custom extended to special guests. The object in his hand is a cola nut about the size of a hard ball, slightly opened on one side to reveal the white nut-meat inside which when chewed apparently produces a considerable chemical stimulus. This prize is offered to Spencer with appropriate ceremony and with the gracious provision that what he does with it after he takes it home is his affair! The Colonel has learned through Spen that Christians avoid some foods or drinks. Spen later makes the most of another opportunity to present the need of a personal Saviour rather than a religion, and our host responds with serious interest. He's a nominal Catholic who is "afraid" to read his Bible; he doesn't want to be confused!

Our journey north from Ika with Spencer and Phyllis, our hosts, to catch our plane for London and Toronto provided time for reminiscing. One personal reflection underlined God's faithfulness in meeting needs both physical and spiritual. The very different Nigerian food, the constantly hot sun each day, the warm nights; the unusual demands in the ministry of the Word (at home, a half hour or so on occasional Lord's Days—here, an hour twice a day for three days, and more on the Lord's Day!), all this provided opportunity for the Lord to show His mercy and grace in His faithfulness to a very needy and thankful helper!

Unlike those of us in Canada, the saints there cannot and do not say that they are rich and have need of nothing. Indeed part of their attractiveness as believers lies in their conscious privation in material things, in contrast to what is too often seen in our land where we pursue material attractions destined for the burning. In addition to the evident needs for electronic hardware and godly medical and other personnel on the station at Ika, there exists a wider and greater need for healing in the fellowship of believers in Nigeria. Dissensions among those who bear the Name of Jesus have resulted in acrimony and open division. And the pagans and Muslims are watching. Recent events in Zaire and Mozambique have encouraged me to hope that God's grace will triumph in Nigeria as well. I am convinced that earnest, concerted and persevering prayer is essential (Colossians 4).

An outstanding impression from six weeks in Nigeria was one of encouragement in glimpsing a part of God's great harvest on this continent. Until this visit, Nigeria had been a blank area on the map of Africa, 'most likely inhabited by uncivilized natives in steaming rain forests, together with malaria-bearing mosquitoes and other unknown threats to life and limb.' Instead, these forests have revealed hundreds and hundreds of godly men and women, rejoicing in the Lord Jesus, and hungry to hear God's Word. Spencer estimates that over 250 assemblies are located within a radius of sixty miles of Ika. Time and time again, as I listened to multiplied hundreds of rich voices of God's people raised in heartfelt praise, the words of the prophet Isaiah 24:16 came to mind: *"From the ends of the earth we hear singing: 'Glory to the Righteous One.'"*

On First Catching Sight of Jerusalem

Israel is a blend of new and old. The old may be seen in ruins dating back to Roman times and beyond and the new in young

Jewish women dressed in army fatigues serving their country alongside their male counterparts.

The nation exists amid threats of extinction from every side. While in the Golan Heights area, I made some uneducated comments to our guide about Israeli radar and their preparedness to intercept incoming enemy planes. Said I in my naivety, "You'll be able to spot them before they get here." His response: "We know when they move on the ground."

Many sites first encountered on arrival in Israel recalled New and Old Testament scenes: on the beach looking out over the Mediterranean Sea, the Western border of ancient and modern Israel; Joppa, the home of the tanner where Peter was staying when he saw the roof-top vision of the sheet let down from heaven containing various animals; the river used by Solomon's men to float logs from the Mediterranean leading up toward Jerusalem where the Temple was to be built (pointed out by our guide, though unrecorded in Scripture); and, further north along the coast, standing on Mount Carmel where Elijah defied the prophets of Baal and proclaimed and demonstrated the reality of Israel's one God in a powerful witness.

It was nearing the end of our stay in Israel. Our bus carried us up the winding road from below sea level at the Dead Sea on up through winding highway and rugged scenery on either side finally to arrive near the outskirts of Jerusalem. We pulled off the highway to a level expanse in the vicinity of the Mount of Olives east of the city. It was here that I first caught sight of the city, *"the city of our God."*

I believe that it is fair to say that I'm not specially attached to shrines of various sorts, whether religious or national. My ethnic roots lie in Northern Ireland, home to both sides of the family for a time before they moved on to Canada. A recent visit to that entrancing land evoked little feeling of attachment to what was now a foreign land. This was different.

"I Never Did Learn to Dance"

My inmost reaction on first catching sight of Jerusalem is difficult to put into words. One central, overwhelming, and lasting impression was that 'This is indeed God's city! Out of all the so-called holy places on the face of our planet, this one city is different.' Here it was that Almighty God had chosen to put His Name, indeed His presence. *"How lovely is your dwelling place, O Lord Almighty,"* exclaims the psalmist, and we might murmur a quiet but heartfelt "Amen!" It's not as though the city is a heap of ruins as are many of the cities of antiquity. It is very much alive and waits expectantly—if cities can so wait expectantly—for the resumption of its glorious destiny. Jerusalem was central to Israel's society in millennia past, and, though for centuries it has been *"trampled on by the Gentiles,"* it will one day be geo-politically central and dominant once again—possibly soon!

Luke, writer of the Gospel of that name, records a fascinating reflection of the response of the Lord Jesus when He with His disciples came up from Jericho to Jerusalem for a final visit to that city, a visit that ended for Him at the cross. The setting for this historic moment may be similar to that chosen by our Jewish guide as noted above. It provides a view of the city from a vantage point above and to the east. Luke records the scene and the Lord's comment: *"As He approached Jerusalem and saw the city, He wept over it and said, 'If you, even you, had only known this day what would bring you peace—but now it is hidden from your eyes.'"* The sight of the city touched a chord deep within the Lord.

We might wonder just how the Lord could 'see the city' as He approached it. It was not the walls that He saw; not the towers; not the gates: *"He saw the city."* When the traveler approaches the city of Jerusalem he does so taking into account the surrounding heights of land. Psalm 125 contains the interesting expression, *"as the mountains surround Jerusalem."* This description is quite true to the topography of the area. When approaching Jerusalem from Jericho as the Lord did and as we did on our tour, you surmount the heights of land to the east of the city and suddenly you look down and there the city in all its beauty lies before and below you. *"It is beautiful in its loftiness, the joy of the whole earth"* (Psalm 48:2). History's pages record the coming of the Roman armed forces under Titus to lay siege to the city and crush Jewish resistance with a massive destruction, all within the lifetime of some of those listening to Jesus that day. Our Lord knew of this coming devastation and it touched His heart.

A Visit to Russia

The Intourist Hotel was our first stop in the city of Yaroslavl. The city on the Volga River boasts a population of about three quarters of a million and a proud history dating back over a thousand years. Ornate Orthodox churches, some in disrepair, dot the city. Seats are not provided for the attendees of these churches. Communist rule for seventy years has not entirely blotted out religion from Russia, though hope seems in short supply. A distinct absence of hope seemed to me to be the legacy of that godless reign. It showed in the faces of the general populace. "We pretended to work and they pretended to pay us," declared our Russian guide.

The foyer of our hotel at our arrival was not all that auspicious. What had evidently been a splendid architectural attraction to welcome the tourist now bore evidence of serious injury: one area of the floor was marked by blood-stains. 'Some problems last night,' was the off-hand explanation. Such a welcome didn't bode well with me. So it was that when I was shown the narrow little room I was to share with Brian Robinson, I wasn't entirely at peace. An underlying anxiety pervaded my thinking as I lay in my narrow bed. I was to spend three months in this 'backward' country and my prayed: 'Lord, I don't mind dying here but don't let me be hospitalized here'! The prospects of a peaceful night were not all that great.

It was sometime in the middle of that night that my troubled sub-conscious roused me into wakefulness. Sleep fled. Brian slept on, in spite of his bed being short for his over six feet of height.

"I Never Did Learn to Dance"

Then it happened. I think of it as a 'visitation.' I wasn't dreaming. Indeed, my senses seemed acutely aware of this phenomenon and of my surroundings. It was as though I were given an awareness of the vast expanse of space over Russia. Though I had no sight of a Presence permeating that space, I did have an inner assurance that this Presence was there and had perfect control of all. Wonderful peace enveloped me and I wept—a rare phenomenon for me—overwhelmed by the transcendence of the experience! Never in my life either before or since have I had such an experience. I didn't talk about it then and very rarely have I mentioned it to anyone since.

A later plan for another visit to Yaroslavl brought a different kind of challenge. The phone call came from Paul Beverly in Russia. After the preliminaries, 'Was it true that I was planning to come to Russia?' Yes. 'Would I consider doing him a favour?' Well . . . What's up? 'Some folks in the States have given some of the Lord's money to the work of the Lord in Russia, and would I consider bringing it with me when I came?' Normal money transfers via banking institutions would encounter problems in Russia. I think I could do that. How much are they sending? '$40,000 US.' Oh! OOH!

The preliminaries attended to, I went to my bank, briefcase in hand, ready to take possession of this fortune in new US $100 bills. (Russians didn't like to accept old bills.) Two ladies of some authority ushered me into the bank manager's office, pulled down the shade of a window facing the street, and proceeded question me about the wisdom of my project. In truth they were quite right to caution me about the wisdom of carrying so much cash at any time in any place, never mind in Russia. Given the right circumstances, a person's life would be worth considerably less than that amount in Russia. Then they opened a package containing eight bundles of bills which they proceeded to count out in my presence. These then were delivered to me and I placed them in my briefcase. They wanted to be informed by my wife when I had safely delivered my treasure.

From that moment I had the sense that people were watching me and that at any time some drastic event might happen. People must know that I was carrying all this ready cash and were waiting an opportunity to relieve me of my burden.

The challenge of going through Russian customs grew as I got near the time. What was I to do with my treasure? The thought occurred to me to spread it around my waist money-belt fashion and so avoid carrying it by hand. Too much like Saul's armor. What was I to say about it?

The crunch came in the Moscow airport when I was required to indicate on Russian Intourist documents how much foreign currency I was bringing with me. I could lie and enter a minimal amount or tell the truth. I had been strengthened to tell the truth before I left Canada when I was led to read about Ezra and his company bringing all the treasure safely through dangerous routes from Babylon and arriving in Jerusalem with all intact. So the decision had been already made to be transparent and trust the Lord.

The person dealing with me took the paper I had filled out. I watched with some trepidation as he glanced over it. Then he wanted to see the cash. I opened my briefcase, and there it was, bundles of new American one hundred dollar bills filling the cavity! I had to stay there while he called his supervisor. I felt quite vulnerable in those moments. The two returned and the process was repeated. They finally approved my entry into the country, and with much relief I closed the case, assembled my other luggage and went to meet Paul on the other side of the barricade. He and a friend with him must have been praying! Relief and thanksgiving were abundant on delivery of the cash to Paul after a hurried exit from the airport through a side door!

"I Never Did Learn to Dance"

On leaving Russia:

Valery had brought me to Moscow and I penned the following note while waiting for my plane:

"A somewhat unusual wave of something akin to nostalgia—almost like a fragrance momentarily sensed during a walk in the forest—wafted over me during the few moments lingering with Valery there in the airport. Before me lay the inevitable customs counters with the bored young men in uniform, and behind me row upon row of Russians chatting with one another. It was these Russian cadences and phrases—more of which I now recognize though many of which I can't translate—it was these that somehow found an inner echo, a resonance, that made me wonder if I had somehow become 'infected' with the soul or spirit of this vast land!

"Surely there is evidence of long endurance of suffering in the psychic scars that mark the spirits of the Russians. One thinks of the current term abuse in this regard. They have been abused by various elements in their national 'body': Tsars that misused their authority and power; the deliverers who promised a new life in a classless society; the religious shepherds who didn't really attend to their task willingly as from the Lord and who failed to reflect the Lord's love for His own."

Ireland, October, 2008

First impressions: The first glimpse of Irish landscape was the rich green of the golf course near Dublin. Other impressions followed: the busy Dublin airport; the construction work on highways etc. heavily subsidized by the European Union; the ubiquitous stone walls, some mortared and some dry; fields cleared and the stones used for fences, walls or for building construction; hours of labour involved, much of it involving skilled workmen, some of it as make-work projects to relieve hardship; remnants of towers round and rectangular, and castles that remain in various states of repair; then there was the deserted village on the side of the mountain, the remnants of houses consisting of four walls but no roofs. The references to the strong tower in the Old Testament make sense in Ireland.

Then too the endless undercurrent of a sense of oppression by English lords of various sorts. It—the Republic—now has its own government, quite at liberty from their former masters; they have their own language, albeit only in part. Irish or Gaelic is seen everywhere in the South, pockets of it hold sway as the common language, mainly in the West, we were told. They are resentful towards the North since they are helped financially to a great extent by the British government. They would like unification of both parts of the island, a legitimate aspiration from their point of view. Goods and traffic flow freely between the two parts even now. They revere their heroes in ballads heartily sung in pubs, men and women who stood up to the British in years gone by. Tale after tale is told of this or that man or woman who lived in this or that village or town and who was distinguished in the cause, even though the outcome was in vain. Sadly, internecine struggles have also made an indelible mark on their past centuries.

Ireland's topography has been accurately and succinctly summed up in Fodor's Exploring Ireland: "The scenery varies from rural pasturelands cut by many rivers, through wild bog lands and low-lying hills, to the most spectacular mountain scenery (mostly in the west and north) sweeping down to the sea in high cliffs and craggy promontories."

My forefathers from both sides of the family passed through Northern Ireland in their pilgrimage from Europe to Canada. Here they found space, freedom and opportunity. By hard work and perseverance they carved out a new life. I don't have the sense that my roots are in Ireland or even in the south of Germany or indeed in Canada, for that matter. "I'm just a-passin' through," as the song says. Moses, who had experience in pilgrimage, sums up the brevity of life as he writes:

"I Never Did Learn to Dance"

*The length of our days is seventy years—
or eighty, if we have the strength;
yet their span is but trouble and sorrow,
for they quickly pass, and we fly away.*

From "A prayer of Moses the man of God" (Psalm 90:10)

    Two or three factors became increasingly evident towards the end of these years of retirement, considerations that seemed to weigh in favour of a possible move from our home of half a century. Our sons had moved on to their own pursuits in life, leaving the empty nest situation with mom and dad. We had significantly enlarged our original house to accommodate a growing family, and now we were left with so much empty space. The fact that the space was used to advantage from time to time when other needs arose did not alleviate the housekeeping burden.

    The reality was that steps and stairs faced the occupants of the home at every turn, and this became more and more of a challenge. Knees that worked well over the past decades now objected to the ups and downs of seemingly endless flights of stairs. One new knee helped, but the challenge was still there.

    We explored the possibility of finding suitable down-sized accommodations on one level with the option of assisted living in nearby Sudbury, but nothing seemed suitable. Then, late one evening, we received a call from Ottawa. It was from David. "We may need the services of a baby-sitter in the near future!" Our focus rapidly changed from Sudbury to Ottawa, together with the joyous prospect of welcoming our first grandchild!

CHAPTER FIVE
Ottawa—"Ripeness is All"

"Men must endure
Their going hence, even as their coming hither:
Ripeness is all."

Edgar - *King Lear* (5, 2, 9)

The move from Onaping Falls to Ottawa was not without a good measure of trauma. Jake, our golden retriever on loan from John, wasn't able to accompany us to the city—and that for a number of reasons: he was getting on in years (fifteen years is old in the life of a golden) and evidences of deterioration of his quality of life had appeared. Furthermore, he wouldn't fit in with condo living, and to think of giving him to another family was not realistic at this stage in his life. Then, of course, the house that had been our home throughout the forty-nine or so years of our marriage had to be sold. Not only so, but the various roots and connections established over the years had to be disturbed, if not severed. Undoubtedly this uprooting and move has had a lasting, deleterious effect, possibly even an unnecessary disturbance, at this stage in our lives. Dr. O'Donohoe's cryptic counsel, "Don't move," may have been a wise option.

Should we have opted for a different choice? Second guessing the outcome had a different choice been made in any particular circumstance seems ill-advised. We only know in part. On the other hand, it may be profitable to re-examine the elements that made up the choice and learn from any mistakes made. Rather than torment oneself with endless 'What if's,' it would seem the path of wisdom to turn from these after learning the lessons and determine that from this day forward such and such will be my purpose.

Frost's lines touch on this theme:

> I shall be telling this with a sigh
> Somewhere ages and ages hence:
> Two roads diverged in a wood, and I,
> I took the one less traveled by,
> And that has made all the difference.

The narrator recognizes that his choice has taken him on a very different path to a different outcome. Is his prophetic sigh one of satisfaction or is it one of regret? At least he succeeds in causing the reader to reflect, and perhaps that is one of the ends of good poetry.

Such reflections are normal as the years add up and needs change. For example, a cursory glance back over my life reveals one curious and unresolved issue. It's like a wound that doesn't heal completely. Plenty of time has elapsed and the question remains outstanding. "What? You still haven't learned to dance?" says the accuser. Here I am at age eighty-five, having been a Christian for well over a half century, and still hesitant to profess what I believe to be true. The evidence is there and increases alarmingly on each social occasion when I am faced with the remark by another Christian: "I love you!" I feel as though I should respond in like manner but some inner constraint inhibits the free reciprocal response.

In my defense I turn to the Scriptures. I find little encouragement there to say to the other person, "I love you." Psalm 18:1 does provide an example of this kind of profession where David says, *"I love you, O Lord, my strength."* Evidently the Hebrew word for love used here is rare in the Old Testament. In the gospel of

"I Never Did Learn to Dance"

John chapter 21 Peter, when pressed into confessing his love for the Lord Jesus, avoids the use of the Greek agape, the word for love that the Lord uses, and instead employs an alternative word meaning, "I'm tenderly affectionate towards you."

The overwhelming biblical direction for Christian believers points to a non-verbal demonstration of love. It is of interest to note that the Lord Jesus at the end of His sojourn on earth says to the disciples, *"As I have loved you, so you must love one another."* When we search the record in John's Gospel of the Lord's interaction with these men over the three years up to this occasion, however, not one instance is given of Him saying to them, "I love you." Yet there is not a question but what He loved them and furthermore showed His love to them on every encounter with them. Years later, this same apostle writes to believers in his time, *"Let us not love with words or tongue but with action and in truth"* (1 John 3:8).

Languages change over time. Some words drop out of use; new words are added. Some words change their value over the years. Other words depend on context to reveal their meaning. The word love is like that. The Concise Oxford Dictionary first defines love as "Warm affection, attachment, likeness or fondness, paternal benevolence, affectionate devotion . . ." The second definition gives "Sexual affection or passion or desire . . ." Three other definitions follow. None of these definitions measures up to the New Testament meaning of love. There, a special word was employed, a word which casts light on the thought of love as God wants the church to know and exercise it. John F. MacArthur in his exposition of 1 Corinthians (see chapter 13) points out the following about this term: "Agape (love) is one of the rarest words in ancient Greek literature, but one of the most common in the New Testament. Unlike our English love, it never refers to romantic or sexual love, for which eros was used, and which does not appear in the New Testament."

I have no recollection of the awareness of the concept of love in the biblical sense in my early years. The oft-quoted and much beloved Bible verse, John 3:16, meant nothing to me either when I read it or heard it. "God so loved the world" might have produced a shrug rather than a recognition of anything familiar in my world. This is not to say that I wasn't loved in those years; no doubt I was, but it's just that I wasn't aware of it and certainly have no recollection of it. Generally speaking, folks of my acquaintance in those days didn't use words to convey their intimate thoughts. On the other hand, they cared for one another and expressed that care in practical ways. If a family suffered a loss of some kind, the neighbours collectively went to their aid. Perhaps it was a cultural thing.

Had I had eyes to see, I would have recognized the many ways in which I was provided for day by day. I ought to have been grateful for 'food and raiment' which came to me abundantly through my father's industry and my mother's care. I wasn't.

By nature I am essentially selfish. There is no doubt that I was selfish as a child, as my father observed one time in those early days in a rare, still-remembered communication from him. I think I come by it honestly—not that I'm pointing the finger at my parents! The culprit, or culprits, rather, lived in the Garden of Eden. Their guidelines for taking decisions leading to actions had to do with self rather than the loving Creator who provided abundantly for them: *"When the woman saw that the fruit of the tree was good for food and pleasing to the eye, and also desirable for gaining wisdom, she took some and ate it."* It was all about "me, myself and I." God and His will didn't enter the equation. The motivation was quite self-centered. Not only so, but her husband was with her in the whole episode, and Adam's extended family continues to this day acting on the basis of what pleases self rather than what pleases God.

God is love.

"It's better felt than tel't," says the old Scot, and there's much homespun wisdom in the adage. Someone has written this interesting note regarding the comprehension of love: "Love can be known only from the actions it prompts." Words alone are inadequate. If you want to convince me that you love me, you'd better demonstrate it. The apostle Paul observes this truth about the love of God being conveyed to us: *"But God demonstrates His own love for us in this: While we were still sinners, Christ died for us"* (Romans 5). John enjoins believers in his day, *"Dear children, let us not love with words or tongue but with actions and in truth"* (1 John 4). It is in God's act of sending His only Son that we see the ultimate demonstration of the love of God. John R. W. Stott comments: "The coming of Christ is, therefore, a concrete, historical revelation of God's love, for love (agape) is self-sacrifice, the seeking of another's positive good at one's own cost, and a greater self-giving than God's gift of His Son there has never been, nor could be." Stott's words call for reflection. God loves *"with actions and in truth"* indeed! Surely the cross is the ultimate, the unequivocal, the culminating action in the demonstration of the love of God.

A most solemn aspect of the reality of the love of God should be noted. To learn of this love and the demonstration of it at the cross and then to spurn it or even neglect it is most solemn indeed and carries the risk of incurring the wrath of God. No other sacrifice exists to bring sinners before God in righteousness. To receive by faith God's love in Christ and His work on the cross is to please God and become heir of all that He has for bankrupt members of Adam's race! The option is most solemn indeed. C. S. Lewis is alleged to have said, "There are only two kinds of people in the end: those who say to God 'Thy will be done', and those to whom God will have regretfully to say, 'Thy will be done.'" How infinitely much better to say to God now, 'Thanks for giving your Son for my sin; I want to do your will.'

Love was the characteristic term for the Christian church in the first century. Tertullian is credited with preserving the comment about the Christians of his day: "See how they love one another!" The night before He left this world for heaven and home, the Lord gave his disciples—and by extension the church—this final command: *"A new command I give you: Love one another."* And, lest we think this command was simply to be added to the six hundred and thirteen existing laws and regulations given to God's people Israel, we read further in 1 John 3:23: *"And this is His command: to believe in the name of His Son, Jesus Christ, and to love one another as He has commanded us."*

The forecast as to the abundance or scarcity of this biblical kind of love at the end of the present age is not all that encouraging. Speaking of conditions to come at that time, the Lord says, *"Because of the increase in wickedness, the love of most will grow cold"* (Matthew 24). Like the rare mineral found occasionally in the mines, agape love would be a rare and precious element at the end of the age. Even while still in the first century the apostle Paul echoes this theme as he speaks of his son in the faith, Timothy: *"I have no one else like him, who takes a genuine interest in your welfare. For everyone looks out for his own interests, not those of Jesus Christ"* (Philippians 2:2f.).

A good friend, when asked for the most important element in the milieu of the meeting of the church, replied without hesitation, "Love!" I cannot think of a more appropriate answer.

"Dear friends," writes the apostle of love (1 John 4:7), *"let us love one another, for love comes from God."*

Retrospection also enables one to discern what appear to be stages in life's journey, though in fact these demarcations may reveal an arbitrarily imposed attempt to bring order out of what may be better described as a continuum. In our part of the globe, the seasons follow each other in orderly procession: spring, the season for birth and new life, is succeeded by summer, a time of growth; then autumn and harvest time arrive; finally wintertime when cold and ice and snow remind us of nature's rest period, waiting for the longer days and warmer sunshine when the annual cycle begins anew.

Nevertheless, these series of cycles of seasons don't go on endlessly; they had a beginning and they will have a conclusion. So we believe! Those whose world view embraces a linear rather than cyclical model for the process of time perceive an ordered progress in events in history. Future events are projected to follow the same pattern. In a more universal context, Sir James Jeans, British physicist, astronomer and mathematician, is reported to have observed that "the universe is running down." The Second Law of Thermodynamics evidently substantiates this way of viewing existence. Shakespeare's Prospero draws "The Tempest" to a close with his prophecy:

> The cloud-capp'd towers, the gorgeous palaces,
> The solemn temples, the great globe itself,
> Yea, all which it inherit, shall dissolve,
> And like this insubstantial pageant faded,
> Leave not a rack behind.

If this is so in the unfolding of successive events on the world stage, it is more evidently so in the individual life. There is a *"time to be born and a time to die,"* says the wise teacher of ecclesiastes. This theme is mirrored in a meditation penned following an outing in the woods:

Reflections from a walk in the forest

In any normal forest—in contrast to a man-made wood lot—one will discover trees in various states of development or decay. Some saplings are to be found, even the odd seedling; other trees at different stages of maturity are there, including a few at full maturity.

Among the mature trees, though not this category exclusively, are to be found specimens that are evidently unhealthy. They have lived and matured and are now beyond their best as to their purpose and design. They have lost their healthy appearance. Their bark and foliage bear witness to a lack of sound health. Some provide necessary sustenance for the woodpeckers as they harvest the worms that have found a home in the weakened tree. Some are leaning precariously, their future in doubt. 'How long till that one comes down?' I ask myself. 'A good wind and it's gone.'

Many lie prostrate in various stages of decay, their life cycle almost complete, as their once firm trunks slowly blend with and become part of the soil from which they grew. Their remains become the source of new forest life.

'Does not nature itself teach you . . .?' asks Paul in the Corinthian letter. And surely it does, if we are willing to take heed.

The wise teacher and author of Ecclesiastes cautioned his readers to remember their Creator while they were still young:

> *Remember Him--before the silver cord is severed,*
> *or the golden bowl is broken;*
> *before the pitcher is shattered at the spring,*
> *or the wheel broken at the well,*
> *and the dust returns to the ground it came from*
> *and the spirit returns to God who gave it.*
>
> Ecclesiastes 12:6, 7

"*Dust you are,*" declared the Creator to the guilty first couple, "*and to dust you will return.*" 'In Bondage to Decay' could be written over all creation.

This is a sad obituary marking the demise of the crowning glory of God's creative work, and things would be dismal indeed for that creation were that the last act in the drama.

Because of the Creator's loving-kindness and because the Son of God came into this scene and gave His life to deal with sin and guilt, we now have a hope, a hope *"that the creation itself will be liberated from its bondage to decay and brought into the glorious freedom of the children of God"* (Romans 8:21).

The trees embody vegetable life and, their life-span completed, they become part of their environment. They don't have spirits, in spite of the teaching of some. We do have spirits, according to the Scriptures, and in fact it might be truer to say that we are spirits, soul-spirits inhabiting bodies. The trees decay and our bodies decay. But the soul-spirit lives on—eternally. That's life, as the saying goes.

"I Never Did Learn to Dance"

'How long till that one comes down?' The sharp thrust of nature's lesson is relentless. I summon courage to look in the mirror of the woods. Decay is there; the witness of the trees is there, but so is hope! That enduring pillar of the gospel, *"He was raised on the third day according to the Scriptures,"* provides a 'sure and certain hope.'

Our sojourn in Ottawa has brought me face to face with my mortality, this threatening consummation of this life, this obstinate reality. Of course I had known theoretically that life here has its limitations, that death happens to all born into Adam's family. I had preached this truth earnestly and solemnly for years. *"It is appointed unto men once to die and after this the judgment,"* I had soberly warned. Our son Peter saw the irony in this turn of events at the time I experienced my first bout with cancer: "Well, Dad, you've been preaching about this for years. Now is your chance to prove it." I quite enjoyed his keen assessment. The cause of this sad verdict is sin inherited from Adam. Its scope is universal. Jesus was the only One to escape this plague and its consequence, yet He came to bear our sin and take our death upon Himself when He went to the cross.

It's one thing to be part of a group, all equally facing the same risk; there's comfort in company. But it's quite another thing to step out of the trench and face the fusillade alone! Now it's my turn. It's like sitting with others in the doctor's office, waiting for the call: "Next!" The tell-tale signs that ought to alert us to the reality of our situation are amusing: the passenger on the bus rises to offer you a seat; thoughtful folks offer you a ride here or there; someone holds the door for you. They recognize the obvious, hidden though such evidence often is from oneself.

Preparations for such a significant event are quite in order. An acquaintance was recently told to set his affairs in order. He was facing serious medical procedures in the immediate future. Isaiah the prophet was sent to King Hezekiah with the sobering message: *"Put your house in order, because you are going to die; you will not live"* (Isaiah 38). I know of a Christian who had evidently experienced some kind of vision—whether waking or sleeping he didn't know—a vision of being caught in a powerful current plunging down rock-strewn rapids. His descent past the threatening rocks was remarkably free of concern or injury, however, as he clearly perceived himself to be held securely and safely in the arms of an unknown but utterly capable Presence beneath him! Such bold assurance as he professed does not spring from mere wishful thinking but has the validation of Scripture: *"The eternal God is your refuge and underneath are the everlasting arms"* (Deuteronomy 33); and again: *"When you pass through the waters, I will be with you"* (Isaiah 43). These assurances were written to God's earthly people for their edification and encouragement in an earlier age, but are equally encouraging for God's people in any age.

    It was about this time that our son John sent us pictures of his descent from the skies above New Zealand after stepping out of the plane into thin air thousands of feet above ground: it turns out that he wasn't alone. He was held securely in the arms of a capable and experienced sky-diver! Just so is the believer held securely in the face of apparent ruin. It was also about this time that my urologist phoned to say that a biopsy from my bladder was positive: it was cancer of the bladder, though by God's mercy "not the invasive kind," he had added. This was in addition to a number of other threats to health and well-being, including Parkinson's, peripheral neuropathy and gall stones that lurked about. Like wolves sensing vulnerability in their prey, these threats circle, waiting the right moment.

    As a society we have learned to employ euphemisms to ease the impact of unattractive, depressing or threatening subjects or events. We've done this when we speak of death, unwelcome as that subject generally is. For example we say about such and such a person that he or she has deceased or that this one has passed on or has passed away. He or she has departed or entered into rest. In a way death is an embarrassment to us for it represents an inglorious end to the grand experiment that is mankind. We can put a man on the moon but we can't keep him alive beyond certain years.

The New Testament employs some helpful euphemisms describing the passage from this life to the next that we customarily call death. Each has its encouraging application. One such term comes from the Greek word *exodos*: it "literally signifies a way out; hence a departure, especially from life." Peter, James and John were with the Lord on the mountain when two *"men, Moses and Elijah, appeared in glorious splendor, talking with Jesus. They spoke about His departure, which He was about to bring to fulfillment."* They talked about Jesus' exodus, His departure from this life, a life that He had been living here for some thirty years. He was departing this scene and going back home! Both Moses and Elijah had long since each made his exodus, Moses through physical decease and Elijah by being caught up in glory. Whether through decease or being caught up in glory, the believer's departure from this scene is essentially an exodus, a way out of this life.

The Christian's exodus, like that of the Twelve Tribes in Egypt, suggests not only a way out but also a liberation, a journey and a future destination. The sojourn of the Twelve Tribes in Egypt turned eventually into slavery as they were forced into bondage by cruel Pharaohs. Their exodus meant deliverance from this bondage and a journey to the 'promised land.' At that time the destination of this delivered company was spoken of as a land flowing with milk and honey, and so it was, though taking possession of it required warfare.

Here in this scene the believer is circumscribed by certain restrictions such as the remnants of the old nature within and the limitations of our humanity without. Paul speaks of this as being part of *"the bondage to decay"* that is the state of creation at present. The exodus we anticipate promises not only a physical departure from this earthly scene but also a deliverance from those limitations that face us here. The believer's destiny is the Father's house, a home already secured for us by the One who has gone on before. That transition will be mind-boggling! No forty-years-long journey through the desert from Egypt to Canaan! We already have our citizenship in heaven's homeland, guaranteed for us through Christ's work on the cross, though the outworking of our sojourn here and the exodus awaits a time yet future. *"But our citizenship is in heaven. And we eagerly await a Savior from there, the Lord Jesus Christ, who, by the power that enables Him to bring everything under His control, will transform our lowly bodies so that they will be like His glorious body"* (Philippians 3).

In the meantime we might benefit by pondering some lessons from that long past exodus. The Israelites spent the night before leaving Egypt in their homes dressed in travel clothing, clearly showing that they were ready for and perhaps eagerly awaiting the journey ahead. Not only so, but while they were waiting they were preoccupied with feasting on roast lamb. Nothing of the lamb was to be left till morning, or if it was, it was to be burned up. Egypt was no place for any part of the sacrificial lamb.

Peter, one of those with the Lord on the mount of transfiguration, wrote later of his own "departure," his "exodus": *"And I will make every effort to see that after my departure you will always be able to remember these things"* (2 Peter 1). The Lord's words and example there on that mountain must surely have been precious to Peter as he neared the time of his own departure.

Another metaphor for death used in the New Testament is translated from the Greek *analuo*: "lit., to unloose, undo, signifies to depart, in the sense of departing from life, a metaphor drawn from loosing moorings preparatory to setting sail . . ." The apostle Paul writes, *"I desire to depart and be with Christ, which is better by far . . ."* (Philippians 1). Later, he employs a similar Greek word to speak of his "departure," his casting off lines that held him close to moorings on this shore: *". . . the time has come for my departure"* (2 Timothy 4:6). He had set his sights on that beckoning shore which lay ahead—glory, with the Lord and, as the Scripture says, *"like Him"*!

"I Never Did Learn to Dance"

Many times at the docks in Tobermory have I witnessed the departure of the ferry going to Manitoulin Island. Typically, as I recall, the ship was held securely at the dock by four lines: two near the bow and two near the stern. When the ship was fully loaded with cars and passengers, the ramps and gangplanks would be retracted, the doors shut and the command given by the skipper standing at the rail by the wheelhouse overseeing all: "Cast off" such-and-such a line; then, "Cast off" this other line, and so on. The lines holding the ship to its moorings would be duly unloosed and the ship freed to set sail. Occasionally he would require one line to remain secure while gentle pressure was applied by the engines causing the stern to ease out from the dock first so as to better position the ship for "setting sail," especially when contrary winds might be an opposing factor.

It is fascinating and at the same time encouraging to observe the "lines" holding my ship to its earthly moorings being unloosed, one at a time! The line of employment that held me fast for years—and that necessarily and thankfully so—has long been unloosed. Then there is the line of travel, the mapping out in firsthand experience of other territories and especially other cultures and, perhaps most interesting of all, other people. Unlikely though it seemed at the time, that line has now been cast off. Then too there is a persistent reluctance to cast off the line of old friends. They, however, have a tendency to 'set sail' before us at any time and so that connection to our earthly moorings becomes easily loosened, if not yet cast off. Our family, our immediate family and our church family, seem the last cable to be cast off. Like the final line of the ferry departing, this may help position us for our departure.

As surely as my departure date looms in the foreseeable future, so surely am I profoundly thankful that my heavenly Captain presides over the casting off process. He was here as a Man and as a Man offered Himself for my sin that He might bring me to His Father in glory. From His vantage point in that glory He oversees all, knows perfectly the hazards implicit in the wind and the current and the shoals. He knows which line to cast off first and which to remain in place until that final move from my earthly moorings. At just the right time the last "line" will be cast off at His command and that breathtaking departure get underway!

The voyage will not be in the least lengthy or tedious. The Bible uses helpful imagery to describe the rapidity of the transition of the believer from this life to the next: *". . . in a flash, in the twinkling of an eye"* (1 Corinthians 15:52). In another passage Paul writes, *"I desire to depart and be with Christ, which is better by far"* (Philippians 1:23). If he wasn't here with the Christians he would be there with the Lord. Tedium or monotony seems far from his mind. The believer is either here or there; the notion of purgatory is not found in the Scriptures. The move from this scene to the presence of the Lord is incredibly fast.

A third euphemism found in the New Testament is from the Greek word *koimaomai*, used in the New Testament ". . . of natural sleep . . . and of the death of the body." Mr. Vine adds this interesting comment about our current English word cemetery: "The early Christians adopted the word koimeterion (which was used by the Greeks of a rest-house for strangers) for the place of interment of their departed; hence the English word 'cemetery,' 'the sleeping place' is derived."

It's an apt metaphor and it refers particularly to the body of the deceased. The invisible part of the person, the soul-spirit, the essence of our being, is no longer present in the earthly dwelling; in the case of the believer he or she is immediately with the Lord which is better by far! Viewing only the body, it seems as though the departed one is at rest, sleeping.

Furthermore, in the case of natural sleep, it is expected that the sleeping one will eventually waken or be wakened. The believer falls asleep here and wakens in glory. One interesting observation comes to mind: though we may recall a bit of tossing and turning of the previous night, we don't remember the moment of falling asleep! It would be a mercy of God were we to experience that which happened to Stephen—at least in his final moment—(he had just finished praying for his persecutors): *"When he had said this, he fell asleep"* (Acts 7:60).

Jairus, a ruler of a synagogue, had a twelve year old daughter, his only daughter, who lay dying. He came to Jesus to ask for help. By the time the Lord got to the ruler's house, the flute players and the mourners were already busy since the girl had died. *"The girl is not dead,"* Jesus said, *"but asleep."* But they laughed at Him. From their point of view they were right; the girl had died. From the Lord's point of view—ultimately the true one—the situation was quite different. Similarly, on hearing of the death of Lazarus, the Lord declared to the disciples, *"Our friend Lazarus has fallen asleep; but I am going there to wake him up."* This was puzzling to them since they understood the Lord's comment to refer to natural sleep. The Lord then clarified the matter by saying plainly, *"Lazarus is dead."*

We have the choice when it comes to point of view. We can, like the mourners at the house of Jairus, choose to look at things strictly from a natural point of view or, while recognizing the natural to be true, we can see as the Lord sees. Abraham chose to believe God, the *"God who gives life to the dead and calls things that are not as though they were"* (Romans 4:17)! Someone has observed that whatever God says about a thing is the truth about it. We too may choose to believe God; He's quite reliable!

And so from that inauspicious beginning in Lions Head nearly eight and a half decades ago, I have arrived in Ottawa, the beautiful Capitol City of Canada. Joan and I now enjoy condo living, a concept unimaginable to us years ago. It is more than a coincidence that Ottawa is also the home of our youngest son, his wife and our only grandchild, Elsa. The other two sons live at some distance—one in Sherbrooke and the other in Bowmanville—both visiting the old folks from time to time and communicating often. Then too the saints at Rideauview Bible Chapel have shown us 'the kindness of God' in their warm welcome.

The intervening years have been replete with learning: learning to survive as an interloper in circumstances where qualifications were lacking; learning to accommodate my 'two left feet' in social circumstances requiring natural graces that seemed lacking. Perhaps such graces merely needed cultivating. And then there was learning in relation to that other parallel sphere about which we know little, the spiritual dimension, the reality that will ultimately prove good, lasting and beautiful! Two interesting findings relating to this spiritual sphere and our fitness to enter there deserve noting: first, all that is in me that belongs to the old creation headed up by Adam, all that relates to fitness for God's presence in that perfect sphere, all this has not improved one iota over the intervening years. Second, that perfect fitness required for God's presence has not changed, nor can it be improved! That fitness is God's gracious provision. Such a fitness is found only in Christ, God's own Son, who paid our sin-debt in full on the cross.

What will that reality be like, that which is 'good, lasting and beautiful'? When planning a trip, one of the more interesting aspects of the preparation is finding out about the destination.

In this case we have to be patient. Curiously, little is said in the New Testament regarding the details of this future abode. The apostle Paul was once caught up to *"the third heaven,"* a place he termed paradise. There he heard inexpressible things, things that man is not permitted to tell (2 Corinthians 12). Perhaps this restriction should wean us from our curiosity about people and things in our future heavenly environment and cause us to focus rather on the one Person we know who will be there and who is at the same time the Centre of all creation!

There is indeed presently a Man in glory, the Man who came from glory two millennia ago to visit this earth and who became like us in every way apart from sin; He it is who gave Himself for us as a sinless offering on the cross of Calvary. Now risen from the dead and seated at the right hand of the Majesty on High, He waits the Father's perfect time to descend earthward again, this

"I Never Did Learn to Dance"

time to call His redeemed ones to meet Him in the air! Then it's homeward bound, to be forever with the Lord in that place He is presently preparing for us: like Him, for Him and with Him to the praise of His glory and for the display of His matchless grace throughout the ages to come.

Amen. Come, Lord Jesus.

CONCLUSION

The foregoing reflections are much like a family photo album. The 'snaps' selected are of interest primarily to those involved in the events at the time the pictures were taken. The ultimate destiny of such an album is predictable: after being dutifully shifted from one shelf to another, it will end up among the rubble in the wastebasket of insignificant history. And that's fine—that's what such wastebaskets are for!

The pleasure was in the making of it, like the pleasure of the potter as his hands and fingers shape the malleable clay; like the pleasure of the turner as the rough wood in his lathe takes pleasing proportions and the rich grain is revealed upon encounter with the sharp blades and appropriate finishes; like the pleasure of the stone mason as the pieces are set into place in appropriate balance, color, texture, size and shape; or like the pleasure evoked as the bare canvass begins to reveal a semblance of the scene in the mind of the painter.

There is something in the consciousness (or sub-consciousness, perhaps) of man that seeks to make sense of existence, an impulse however deep within the psyche that longs to give meaning to the oft-perceived formlessness and futility of life. Evidently our earth could at one time be described as *"formless and empty,"* and at some point the Creator was moved to speak and bring in form and fullness, beauty and order. In so doing He found pleasure in His work.

CPSIA information can be obtained at www.ICGtesting.com
Printed in the USA
LVOW13s2248200414

382514LV00001B/54/P